United States
Department of
Agriculture

Forest Service

Southern
Research Station

General Technical
Report SRS–110

Synthesis of Knowledge of Hazardous Fuels Management in Loblolly Pine Forests

Douglas J. Marshall, Michael Wimberly, Pete Bettinger, and John Stanturf

A SUMMARY OF
KNOWLEDGE FROM THE

Joint
Fire Science
Program

Authors:

Douglas J. Marshall, Research Professional, Warnell School of Forestry and Natural Resources, University of Georgia, Athens, GA 30602 (djm2427@warnell.uga.edu); **Michael Wimberly**, Associate Professor, Geographic Information Science Center for Excellence, Wecota Hall, South Dakota State University, Brookings, SD 57007 (Michael.Wimberly @sdstate.edu); **Pete Bettinger**, Associate Professor, Warnell School of Forestry and Natural Resources, University of Georgia, Athens, GA 30602 (pbettinger@warnell.uga.edu); **John Stanturf**, Research Ecologist, Center for Forest Disturbance Science, U.S. Forest Service, Southern Research Station, Athens, GA 30602 (jstanturf@fs.fed.us).

Cover photos courtesy of Joseph J. O'Brien (left)
and Dale W. Wade (top and bottom right)

November 2008

Southern Research Station
200 W.T. Weaver Blvd.
Asheville, NC 28804

Synthesis of Knowledge of Hazardous Fuels Management in Loblolly Pine Forests

Douglas J. Marshall, Michael Wimberly, Pete Bettinger, and John Stanturf

Preface

In recent years, the danger of destructive wildfires has become a major problem in many areas of the United States due to an increase in the human population and to decades of fuel accumulation resulting from wildfire suppression and climatic variability. Fencing of livestock has also reduced the frequency of woods burning to improve livestock grazing. As a result, forests that previously burned regularly have been allowed to build up so much fuel so that when a wildfire does occur, it can be intense and difficult to suppress, endangering lives and property and degrading the forest. A series of major wildfires in the West and in Florida during the late 1990s highlighted the problem and provided the catalyst for new, aggressive government strategies for reducing hazardous fuel levels. The Cohesive Fuels Strategy (U.S. Department of the Interior and U.S. Forest Service 2006) and the Healthy Forests Initiative (U.S. Department of the Interior 2006a) have accelerated the rate of hazardous fuel reduction through administrative reform, new legislation, and increased funding. The mandate of the Healthy Forests Initiative was to reduce fuels to the point where subsequent management by means of regular, low-intensity prescribed burns would be effective. Treatment of forests near buildings and roads (at the wildland-urban interface) was to be emphasized. Subsequently, government agencies increased their fuel reduction activities, especially the use of mechanical equipment to either mulch fuels or remove them from the forest. According to the October 2006 Healthy Forest Report (U.S. Department of the Interior 2006b), Federal agencies have reduced the wildfire hazard on over 18 million acres since 2000. Based on accomplishment reports, the Federal government treated over 3 million acres of the wildland-urban interface and over 1 million acres of other land in the South. For both areas, prescribed burning was the most common treatment.

Complementing the work of the Healthy Forest Initiative is the Joint Fire Science Program, which is a collaboration among six Federal agencies to provide scientific information in support of fuel and fire management programs. In 2005, the Program funded research to develop Knowledge Syntheses for hazardous fuel management in forest types that are characterized by:

- A broad geographic coverage
- A significant wildland-urban interface
- A susceptibility to destructive insect outbreaks
- A set of ecosystems with high political and public interest
- A potential for smoke problems and air quality issues
- A potential susceptibility to invasive species

For the South, loblolly pine (*Pinus taeda*) meets all of these criteria, and this synthesis is intended to serve as a general overview of hazardous fuels in loblolly pine-dominated forests as well as a reference guide to different fuel management treatments. Other types of southern pine forests, including those dominated by slash pine (*Pinus elliottii*) and longleaf pine (*Pinus palustris*), will be covered in other syntheses. However, selected examples of fuel management from these forest types are discussed in this publication where the information is relevant to loblolly pine forests. The synthesis is not designed to be a manual on recommended treatments. Rather, information is provided to allow readers to understand which treatment options are feasible, what the approximate expected costs would be, and how treatments might affect fuels and non-fuel factors such as soil, water quality, and wildlife. Readers are given enough information to decide what options should be explored in greater detail through other publications or consultation with professionals.

This synthesis relies heavily on anecdotal information in addition to published works. Southern fuel reduction operations are rarely documented and while some land managers informally exchange information on such operations, many are not familiar with previous operations and what was learned. This lack of documentation and limited information exchange was a major incentive for the development of this and other fuel management syntheses. During the development of this synthesis, various private and public land managers were interviewed about their fuel management techniques and experiences, with an emphasis on finding new or more effective ways of dealing with fuels as well as identifying operational issues that may not be obvious (e.g., contract terms, soils). Therefore, some of the information provided in this synthesis is derived from the scientific literature (and identifiable by literature citations), while other information is noted as being derived from personal communications. In some cases we summarize anecdotal information from our visits with forest managers and operators. The latter is done in an attempt to avoid providing explicit costs, such as contracted prices, incurred in specific operations.

CONTENTS

Synthesis of Knowledge of Hazardous Fuels Management in Loblolly Pine Forests

Douglas J. Marshall, Michael Wimberly, Pete Bettinger, and John Stanturf

Abstract

This synthesis provides an overview of hazardous fuels management in loblolly pine (*Pinus taeda*) forests, as well as a reference guide on prescribed burning and alternative fuel management treatments. Available information is presented on treatment feasibility, approximate costs, and effects on soil, water quality, and wildlife. The objectives of fuel management in loblolly pine forests are to reduce the density of some targeted plant vegetation and change the structural condition of the forest, or both. Prescribed burning is the most common tool for managing fuels in the South due to the relatively low cost per acre and the ability to reduce fuel levels rather than rearrange them. Mechanical treatments may be effective in reducing wildfire risk by redistributing the fuels closer to the ground, creating a more compact fuel bed. Mulching (mastication) and chipping are the only common mechanical treatments in the Southern United States and generally are used as precursors to prescribed burning. The limited use of mechanical treatments is due to the rapid redevelopment of live fuels and higher treatment costs than prescribed burning. Herbicide treatments for hazardous fuels management are a realistic option in certain situations. Although herbicides cannot replace prescribed burning or mechanical operations where dead fuels must be removed or repositioned closer to the ground, they are useful as preliminary treatments to kill or suppress live fuels or following a prescribed burn or mechanical operation to kill resprouting woody species. Although livestock grazing is no longer common in southern forests, grazing can be used to reduce certain types of live fuels. For example, sheep grazing has been used in Florida to control saw palmetto (*Serenoa repens*). Wider impacts of fuel treatments are discussed for several social and ecological factors, such as soil erosion, water quality, wildlife, and public acceptability.

Keywords: Chipping, hazardous fuels, herbicides, mechanical treatments, mulching, prescribed burning.

Introduction

The loblolly pine (*Pinus taeda*) forests of the South and the wildfires that occur in them do not lend themselves to easy ecological classification because of the influence of human land use on the region. The extent and importance of loblolly pine forests are largely consequences of agricultural abandonment, forest management, wildfire suppression, and the extensive use of prescribed burning. The majority of wildfires in the South are started by humans, and wildfire

occurrence is exacerbated by the rapidly expanding population and the way that new housing is often built adjacent to loblolly pine forests. Thus, southern forest management must take into account the broader landscape context of a particular management unit. Furthermore, changing forest land ownership patterns indicate a growing proportion of small parcels in which hazardous fuel management is problematic. To clarify the complex interactions among loblolly pine, humans, and hazardous fuel management, we will review the history of the southern forests and how loblolly pine came to become the dominant pine species in the region. In addition, we will discuss the population growth in the South, the growing wildland-urban interface, and evolving land ownership patterns.

Photo courtesy of Dale W. Wade

History of Southern Forests

At the time of European arrival, most major southern vegetation communities were produced by the interaction among species adaptations, natural disturbances, and Native American agricultural and fire practices. The Native Americans regularly used fire around their settlements (Stanturf and others 2002), and the landscape was a mosaic of savanna-like longleaf pine (*Pinus palustris*) forest (resulting from lightning-ignited fires) interspersed with lowlands, and the ecotone between the two contained substantial amounts of loblolly pine forest. Apart from limited observations by early Spanish explorers, the earliest European and American descriptions of the southern landscape date from the 19th century, by which time the Native American influence had been declining for over a century, and the majority of the region had been depopulated by disease and warfare. While travelers wrote of large expanses of longleaf pine-dominated savannas, their travels were limited in scope, and systematic study of the southern landscape would not occur until the early 20th century. Even now, the extent and composition of pre-European forests remain unclear. Utilizing old government and personal accounts to estimate the pre-European range of longleaf pine, Frost (1993) estimated that longleaf-dominated forests and savannas covered 93 million acres in the pre-European South while pine-hardwood and slash pine (*Pinus elliottii*) forests covered another 13 million acres.

While details about the pre-European forests will likely remain unknown, it is known that until the arrival of steam-powered equipment, the majority of post-European forests were unlogged mature pine-dominated stands that were burned regularly by local farmers and herdsmen. Conner and Hartsell (2002) estimated that in 1630 (after the decline of Native American populations and before large-scale clearing), southern pine and hardwood forests covered 354 million acres in vegetation patterns similar to those found in the early 19th century. Starting in the late 19th century, railroad technology freed loggers from a dependence on large rivers for log transport. At the same time, the growing market for lumber as well as the success of cash crops such as tobacco and cotton encouraged large-scale logging and conversion to farms. By 1927, only 12.6 million acres of the original 121 million acres of pre-European pine forests remained (Schultz 1997) [Due to differences in methodologies, the pre-European estimates provided by Schultz (1997) and Frost (1993) do not match]. Poor farming practices, the cotton boll weevil (*Anthonomus grandis*), and the Great Depression forced many small farmers off their lands, and these areas were left to revegetate on their own. Since loblolly pine is a prolific seeder and was often left in depressions or along property boundaries, it quickly colonized these abandoned areas. In addition, Federal Depression-era work programs, such as the Civilian Conservation Corps, planted large areas with loblolly pine and slash pine seedlings for soil conservation. This revegetation produced the second forest of the South, which would form the foundation of the future southern forestry industry. The disturbance history of pine forests may have changed as well, as certain State laws, such as Georgia's O.C.G.A. § 4-3-3 "Permitting livestock to run at large or stray" (State of Georgia 2006. Title 4. Animals; Chapter 3. Livestock running at large or straying; § 4-3-3. Permitting livestock to run at large or stray. State of Georgia, Atlanta, GA), which was enacted in 1953, encouraged landowners to fence their property and caused a major reduction in the frequency of woods burning.

The Modern Southern Forests

The total forest area of the South has remained fairly stable since 1982. Conner and Hartsell (2002) estimate that there were about 215 million acres of forests in 1999, versus 218 million acres in 1982. Additions to forest land started to exceed removals by 1987, reversing a long-term trend. However, the increase is fairly small in comparison with the total forest acreage. Recently, Florida and Louisiana have been losing forest area while Alabama, Arkansas, Mississippi, and Kentucky have been gaining it (Wear and Greis 2002).

Of the 200 million acres of timberland in the South (forests with sufficient wood for potential harvesting) in 1999, 52 percent was in hardwoods, 25 percent in loblolly pine-shortleaf pine (*Pinus echinata*), 7 percent in longleaf pine-slash pine, and 15 percent in oak-pine (Conner and Hartsell 2002). The uplands of the Coastal Plain and lower Piedmont are dominated by pines, while the upper Piedmont, Appalachian Mountains, Cumberland Plateau, and Lower Mississippi Alluvial Valley are dominated by hardwoods. While the hardwoods are largely naturally regenerated, 48 percent of the pine forests were planted. Another important characteristic of the pine forests of the South is their age structure. Most planted stands are harvested by age 30 to 40. There was 30 million acres of planted pine in the South in 1999; of this area, 89 percent was in pines < 28 years old and one-half was in pines < 13 years old (Conner and Hartsell 2002).

The History, Current Distribution, and Economic Importance of the Loblolly Pine

The age structure and geographic distribution of southern forests have important implications for loblolly pine and its connection with fuels and wildfire. Loblolly pine is one of the most widespread and important tree species in the South, but its widespread dominance and economic significance are actually fairly recent developments. As mentioned earlier, it is believed that during the last few centuries of the pre-European era, most of the Coastal Plain uplands were dominated by longleaf pine and kept in savanna-like conditions by frequent fires set by Indians and lightning, with loblolly pine and slash pine thought to have been confined to the moist zone between the droughty, fire-prone uplands and the hardwood-dominated wet bottomlands (Stanturf and others 2002). Historically, loblolly pine also existed as a co-dominant species with longleaf and shortleaf pine on upland sites in the Coastal Plain, and was common in pine and pine-hardwood stands across the Piedmont and to east Texas, beyond the natural range of longleaf pine.

Like most southern pines, loblolly pine is adapted to colonizing recently disturbed areas where the soil has been exposed. Loblolly pine seeds are light and can travel a long distance. Once seeds germinate, the seedlings can grow rapidly despite harsh conditions. However, while loblolly pine are fire-tolerant once they reach a certain size, seedlings have less resistance to fire, and trees need to reach about 5 to 10 feet tall to survive a fire. That is why loblolly pine was historically restricted to the mesic (wet) margins, even though it grows faster than longleaf pine, which is tolerant of the drier conditions of the more pyric (associated with burning) upland areas. In the Piedmont, loblolly pine was confined to

wet depressions since it could not outcompete the hardwoods in wet areas or shortleaf pine in the drier areas (Stanturf and others 2002). Because it has value as a forestry species and is adaptable to different soils and climates, loblolly pine is now grown from Delaware to Florida and east Texas (fig. 1).

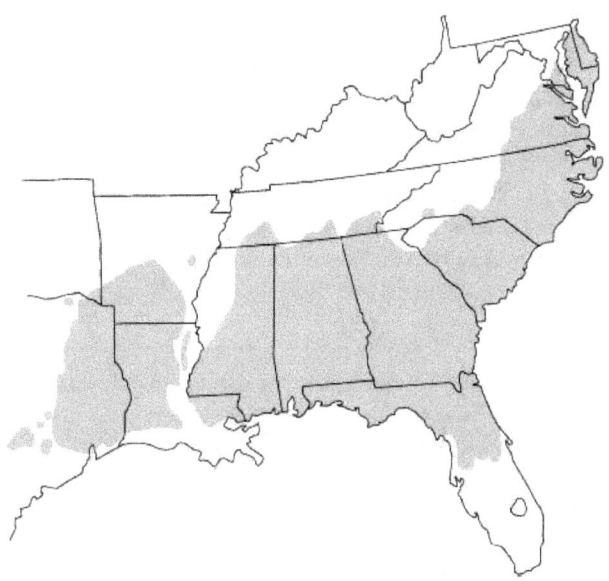

Figure 1—Current range of loblolly pine (*Pinus taeda L.*) in the Southern United States. (U.S. Forest Service map)

It is not possible to associate loblolly pine with any particular soil type, although it is unlikely to be found in excessively well-drained or poorly-drained soils, mainly because of high nutrient demands rather than soil moisture relations. Similarly, loblolly pine is not found exclusively in any particular plant community, although naturally maintained populations do require periodic major disturbances to give seedlings an advantage over hardwoods. The advantage of loblolly pine over slash pine for intensive forestry is in greater fusiform rust (*Cronartium fusiforme*) resistance, higher juvenile growth rates, and better responsiveness to cultural treatments such as fertilizer and competition control. Loblolly pine is also more resistant to ice damage, another reason why it is preferred north of the natural range of slash pine.

Since the 1950s, forestry has been an important part of the southern economy. Abt and others (2002) found that by 1997, the wood products-based sector accounted for about 5.5 percent of southern jobs and 6 percent of the gross regional product. Outside of the slash pine-dominated flatwoods of north Florida, loblolly pine is the most important species for southern forestry.

Forest Land Ownership Patterns

The bulk of southern forest land has always been in private hands. Many large tracts were created during the Great Depression to provide hunting or forest products. One project of the Civilian Conservation Corps, for example, was planting trees. In 1999, 89 percent of the 200 million acres of timberland in the South was privately owned (Conner and Hartsell 2002). Birch (1997) estimated that there were 4.9 million ownership units. There were 3.13 million acres of loblolly and shortleaf pine in southern national forests and 2.20 million acres in other public ownership in 2002 (Smith and others 2004). The nature of southern land ownership has important implications for potential fuel management treatments since owners have different objectives and constraints on the management of their land.

Large forested tracts are typically managed for forest products or game species, and are usually pine forests. However, patterns of ownership of large tracts have been changing over the last few decades. Fifty-four percent of southern plantations (by area) are now owned by corporations, and sales of land to investment fund companies by traditional forestry companies are increasing (Stanturf and others 2003a). From 1982 to 1999, investment companies increased their land base by 20 percent to 20 million acres. Also, in certain high population growth areas, forestry companies are selling large tracts of land for development.

While the total forest acreage (all owners) does not appear to have changed much since 1982, there have been significant changes in tract sizes. Birch (1997) found that between 1978 and 1994, both the total number and total acreage of private forest land tracts increased while average tract size decreased. These trends reflect the growing number of individual landowners who buy forest land as an investment, and the desire of people to move further away from urban centers. One of the most important consequences is the increase of small housing tracts adjacent to larger forested tracts in rural areas, an important characteristic of the wildland-urban interface.

The Wildland-Urban Interface and Fire

According to the 2000 Census, the U.S. population increased 13 percent during the previous decade to over 281 million (Perry and Mackun 2001). The West and South grew much faster (20 and 17 percent), than the Midwest and Northeast (8 and 6 percent) and the southern population increased to over 100 million, accounting for 36 percent of the total U.S. population. Accompanying this rise in population was a general increase in housing development in rural areas, especially near major urban centers. From 1982 to 1992, 6.5 million acres in the South were converted from rural to urban population densities, with highest rates of conversion in Texas, Georgia, Florida, and North Carolina (Cordell and Macie 2002). This conversion is the basis for the growth in the wildland-urban interface, which now ranges from 5 percent in Texas to 44 percent in North Carolina (Radeloff and others 2005).

For most cases, the wildland-urban interface can be considered a mix of rural features (forests and agriculture) and urban ones (high road and housing densities) where there is an increased risk for wildfire ignition and spread, and an increased risk of damage to features valued by humans. The wildland-urban interface is an important area for fuel management, and its definition is commonly based on housing units per unit area. However, as pointed out by Wimberly and others (2006), it is more realistic to consider the wildland-urban interface as a dynamic group of social, physical, and biotic gradients. For example, a southern wildland-urban interface could range from isolated recreational cabins to dense subdivisions. Thus, in this guide, the wildland-urban interface will be treated as a general concept rather than specific set of conditions.

While the nature of the wildland-urban interface is somewhat vague, its importance in the fuel management discussion is clear. As will be discussed in the next section, the majority of southern wildfires are caused by debris burning and arson. This means that there is a two-way wildfire risk relationship in these areas, as wildfires are most likely to start where residential areas are adjacent to forests. At the same time, the density of homes and their proximity to fuel sources suggests that once a wildfire starts, it can quickly spread to the houses and cause a large amount of damage in a small area. Thus, both firefighters and foresters consider protecting homes from wildfire a high priority.

An important consideration in protecting homes is the size and location of nearby forest tracts. In many areas of the wildland-urban interface, loblolly pine forests are broken up into small forested tracts intermixed with residential tracts. As a forest tract decreases in size, it becomes more difficult and expensive to manage fuels in that tract given the economy of scale for forestry treatments such as thinning or prescribed burning (Greene and others 1997). Treatments have certain fixed costs regardless of the total acreage treated (e.g., move-in costs), so the cost per acre generally increases as tract size decreases. Mechanical treatments, for example, may suffer from these economies of scale, but they may be the only option where prescribed burning is precluded for other reasons. However, the renewed interest in forest biofuels may change the economics associated with these treatments.

The increase in the area of wildland-urban interface and changing social values in an urban-dominated society are often cited as major impediments to hazardous fuel management (Stanturf and others 2003b), particularly where prescribed burning is considered. However, Loomis and others (2001) conducted a phone survey of Florida residents and found that the majority considered prescribed burning acceptable. Most southern State governments have also passed legislation specifically designed to promote prescribed burning, although Haines and others (2001) found that the most important limitations to burning operations were State-level smoke (i.e., air quality) regulations, personnel limitations, and legal liability.

Fire and Fuel Issues

We will consider loblolly pine forests not as a distinct habitat, but as a gradient of growing conditions and plant species compositions, with loblolly pine as the dominant overstory species. Likewise, the fuel conditions found in these forests vary according to tree and understory species composition, growth and decomposition rates, stage of succession, past management practices, and other factors. Therefore, to effectively deal with fuels and wildfire risk under these varying conditions, managers should treat each forest as unique and be adaptable to different management options.

Wildfire in the South

Occurrence—While the yearly occurrence of wildfires in western forests is well known due to their severity and difficulty to suppress, the 13 Southern States actually have far more wildfires than the 15 Western States, according to the National Interagency Fire Center (2006a). The vast majority of southern wildfires are caused by humans, and human-caused wildfires burn more acreage, in total, than do others.

Although the South has more wildfires than other regions of the country, these fires are usually smaller due to forest fragmentation and easy access, so initial attack is often effective. For example, in Georgia, while there are about 8,700 wildfires annually, they average < 5 acres in size (Georgia Forestry Commission 2006). Similarly, the average Arkansas wildfire is about 14 acres (Personal communication. 2005. M. Cagle and L. Nance, Staff

Forester and Deputy State Forester, Arkansas Forestry Commission, 3821 West Roosevelt Rd., Little Rock, AR 72204). From 1997 to 2005, there were 43 U.S. wildfires of at least 100,000 acres, but only one (the 1998 Volusia complex wildfire in North Florida) was in the South (National Interagency Fire Center 2006b). In 2007, however, the largest wildfire in the United States occurred in and around the Okefenokee Swamp in southern Georgia and northern Florida (for administrative purposes this complex was managed as three separate fires, the Sweat Farm Road, Big Turnaround, and Bugaboo). Nevertheless, the annual probability of a southern forest having a wildfire appears to be very low. Zhai and others (2003) analyzed data from 17,534 south-central permanent inventory plots that were measured from 1988 to 1992 and found that within the previous two years of measurement, 0.2 percent of the plots had been burned by wildfire, 3.3 percent had been prescribed burned, and 0.9 percent had been burned by unidentified factors. Thus, a conservative estimate for wildfire probability for the South-Central United States could be 0.5 percent per year.

Causes of wildfire—Wildfire data collected by State forestry agencies indicates that the majority of wildfires in the South are caused by debris burning (e.g., burning of yard wastes) and arson. For example, in Georgia, debris burning was responsible for 51 percent of the wildfires while arson was responsible for an additional 18 percent (Georgia Forestry Commission 2006). Similarly, 43 percent of Arkansas wildfires were caused by arson and 30 percent by debris burning (Arkansas Forestry Commission 2006). However, the situation is different in Florida, where arson, debris burning, and lightning accounted for 25 percent, 19 percent, and 19 percent of wildfires respectively (Florida Division of Forestry 2004). Furthermore, Florida has a pronounced lightning season (May–October) during which lightning becomes the dominant ignition source.

Types of wildfire—In the South, wildfires can move slowly through the organic layers of soils (duff-related fires), near the surface of the ground, or in the crowns of trees. In coastal parts of the Carolinas, thick organic soils can increase problems associated with duff-related fires during dry conditions. Organic soils do not burn intensely, but they can burn for many days and produce large amounts of smoke. Heavy accumulations of duff have the potential to cause serious problems in some southern pine forests, in terms of mop-up effort required, potential smoke production, and danger associated with re-ignition. Forest fragmentation and longer time intervals between fires only increase the threat. During droughty years, the risk of damage to tree roots may be increased in duff fires.

Surface fire is a common type of wildfire. In surface fires the midstory and understory vegetation are consumed, and the overstory canopy (crown) does not burn except under unusual wind and drought conditions. Although crown fires are relatively rare even during severe wildfire seasons, surface fires can generate enough heat to damage overstory trees through scorching or thermal girdling. For example, the 1998 wildfire season in North Florida was unusually intense and destructive due to an extended drought and a string of arson attacks and lightning strikes. Outcalt and Wade (2004) examined burned slash pine stands in Osceola National Forest and found that even though the wildfires had killed about 30 to 50 percent of trees, crown fire had been relatively rare. In most stands, only 10 to 20 percent of the plots had at least 75 percent crown scorch (in which the heat from a fire singes the leaves and needles in the top branches of trees), which included some cases of crown fire (where fire spreads to the top branches of the trees). Crown fires were not common in stands that had been prescribed burned regularly but were fairly common in stands that had not been prescribed burned.

What are Hazardous Fuels?

Wildfires in the South are often situated near buildings and roads and can cause large amounts of property damage and injury in a small area. In addition, since the wildland-urban interface is rapidly expanding, wildfire danger has to be considered both for existing homes and infrastructure and for expected future development. Furthermore, different land managers have different protection priorities, varying from endangered species to water quality to recreational visitors. Hence, the concept of hazardous fuels is a matter of interpretation and objectives and does not easily lend itself to definition. Background about forest fuel concepts as they relate to fire behavior and intensity is provided in the appendix.

Fuel management objectives will vary by location, protection priorities, budgetary resources, and the long-term management goals of each landowner. The most common fuel management objective is to manipulate forest vegetation in order to reduce the potential for severe wildfires. Another common objective is to manipulate forest vegetation in order to form a protective barrier around a stand or resource. The main idea behind a fuel management treatment in a loblolly pine forest is either to reduce the density of some targeted species of vegetation, or to effectively change the structural condition of the forest. A number of techniques can be employed to accomplish this, including thermal (prescribed burning), mechanical, chemical, and biological methods.

Fuel Treatment Techniques

Prescribed Burning

Overview—Prescribed burning is the most commonly used tool for managing fuels in the South because it has relatively low cost per acre and reduces fuel levels rather than just rearranging them. There are four general firing techniques for prescribed burning, and the choice of which to use should be made based on the objectives of the burn, the fuels present, the topography of the area, and the weather conditions. Wade and Lunsford (1989) provide land managers a guide for using prescribed burning in southern forests, so discussion of firing techniques is limited here. The basic firing techniques described in the prescribed burning guide include: (1) back fires, which are slow moving and result in minimum residual tree scorch; (2) head fires, which are fast moving and result in good smoke dispersal; (3) flank fires, which are relatively moderate in speed and useful for securing the edges of a burned area; and (4) spot fires, which can have characteristics of the other three techniques depending on the density of the ignition grid, the topography, and weather conditions.

If a stand has an open canopy, prescribed burning every 2 to 3 years encourages early successional herbaceous species at the expense of woody ones. However, prescribed burning is also an imprecise practice that can quickly turn from beneficial to destructive with unexpected weather changes or fuel conditions. Furthermore, offsite smoke can lead to automobile accidents as well as air quality problems. The legal liabilities associated with these offsite problems and the logistical difficulties of burning near roads and buildings are major concerns. Consequently, the long-term use of prescribed burning in some areas of the South is becoming questionable due to restrictions on burning near dense housing and roads, and it is likely that some current burning programs will become too costly or otherwise infeasible within the next 20 years, regardless of the intent of the landowner. However, in many parts of the South, social and economic conditions still allow the regular use of prescribed burning and probably will continue to do so for the next few decades.

Until the last few decades, the South was predominately a rural region where the burning of fields and forests was an accepted cultural practice. Prescribed burning is still used in loblolly pine forests to prevent fuel accumulation and encourage forage for game species. However, relative to the total area of forests, prescribed burning is not common in most Southern States outside of the Coastal Plain pine forests. For example, an average of approximately

900,000 acres are prescribed burned every year in Alabama (Alabama Forestry Commission 2005), which represents 4 percent of the total forest area of about 23 million acres. In Arkansas, about 300,000 acres are treated each year (Personal communication. 2005. M. Cagle and L. Nance, Staff Forester and Deputy State Forester, Arkansas Forestry Commission, 3821 W. Roosevelt Rd., Little Rock, AR 72204), or 2 percent of the 18.8 million acres of forest land. In contrast, an average of 2 million acres are prescribed burned in Florida every year (Florida Division of Forestry 2006), or 14 percent of the total 14.7 million acres of forest land, while an average 300,000 acres are burned by wildfires. These Florida numbers reflect the presence of fire-prone flatwoods, the importance of lightning and humans as ignition sources, and aggressive programs of prescribed burning by private and public land managers.

Feasibility—There are many factors to be considered when deciding if prescribed burning should be used for fuel reduction. While most constraints will not automatically preclude the practice, some problems may be serious enough to make it infeasible. Issues such as forest management objectives, the long-term accumulated costs of regular treatments, and the expected future development of the surrounding lands must be taken into account. Even if prescribed burning is desired and fuel conditions are favorable, constraints from outside the property can effectively preclude the practice. Another important consideration is legal liability. In areas where land is being developed for residential and other uses, large landowners are eliminating prescribed burning as a management practice because of the associated liability.

Many Southern States have established legal protection for prescribed burning with regard to damage outside the property, but the protection is not absolute and there is always some potential for legal action. This increased protection is often based on having State-certified professionals in charge of the burning and generally does not apply to non-certified burners. Finally, prescribed burning may be incompatible with fertilization programs, as recent pre-burn applications of nitrogen treatments can be wasted through volatilization.

Roads—Excessive smoke must not be allowed to reach major roads and intersections, which means a specific set of weather conditions is required. The presence of major roads does not automatically preclude prescribed burning, but it does introduce additional restrictions that may ultimately make prescribed burning impractical. If there are only one or two stretches of roads to be considered, then it may be possible to burn in a way that keeps smoke away from the roads. However, as the extent of roads to be avoided increases, it becomes more and more unlikely that the necessary weather conditions will occur often enough to make regular burning a practical management option. Conversely, a lack of access roads may make prescribed burning dangerous if there is limited ability to move people and equipment to trouble spots.

Firebreaks—Related to the issue of access roads is the presence of firebreaks. The construction of firebreaks can represent a major investment, although some State agencies will build them for private landowners at a reduced cost. Once constructed, the firebreaks will need regular upkeep, and thus to be effective will require a periodic investment.

Housing and other sensitive areas—Like the surrounding road system, housing and other sensitive areas represent a potential limitation. While some neighbors may be willing to tolerate smoke if given prior warning, others may be less accommodating. Another important issue is the danger created by the landscaping activities of neighboring landowners, as where homes are surrounded by trees or other flammable material. It is the responsibility of the person performing the burn to protect neighboring properties from escaped prescribed burns even if the neighbors allow large amounts of flammable material to accumulate near their homes or other improvements such as utility poles, telephone pedestals, and gas lines.

Another important issue is the presence of smoke-critical areas, such as schools, airports, or homes with elderly people (fig. 2), where any level of smoke is unacceptable. Smoke can be kept away from these critical areas, as it can be kept away from roads, by burning under specific weather conditions. If the surrounding area near some forest of interest is being developed, then the long-term prospect of being able to maintain a prescribed burning program in that forest is likely to be questionable.

Topography—Serious public relations problems can arise when burning is conducted in areas where topography can trap smoke. Such areas include drainages that funnel ground-level smoke as well as hills or mountains that trap rising smoke. River bottoms with bridges are an especially important danger area. These types of topography do not automatically preclude the use of prescribed burning, but certain weather conditions are necessary when they are present.

Concurrent burning operations—The presence of other burning activity in the area can present both possible limitations and benefits. For example, prescribed burning

Figure 2—High-density housing next to Jones State Forest in Texas. (Photo courtesy of Douglas J. Marshall)

programs can compete with each other for opportunities to conduct burns under favorable conditions, but if surrounding lands are being burned, all parties may gain by coordinating and sharing their resources and fire barriers. In Georgia, the Forestry Commission essentially acts as the unofficial prescribed burning coordinator, but in the other Southern States, it may be the individual controlled-burn managers who make sure that there are not too many prescribed burns in one area.

Legal issues—Concern about legal liability is a major limitation to the use of prescribed burning. While most Southern States have laws designed to encourage the practice, many of these laws are unclear about what is legally required and when a burner is legally protected. While many State forestry agencies have the prescribed burning laws posted on their Internet sites, these sites provide little, if any, interpretation of the laws, and landowners must decipher the legal complexities on their own. Haines and Cleaves (1999) and Sun (2006) provide general reviews of State laws on prescribed burning. However, liability varies based on onsite and offsite factors, the amount of fire and smoke damage, the presence or absence of a State-certified prescribed burn manager, and the

preventive measures that were taken. Landowners who have little experience with prescribed burning and the associated legal environment are advised to contact the appropriate State agency for guidance.

Air quality—For prescribed burning, the most important air quality standards are for (a) air-borne particles that are small enough to enter the lungs and cause health problems, and (b) smoke conditions that reduce the vision of drivers. The issue for prescribed burners is to determine what burning restrictions have been implemented in their particular counties. The Environmental Protection Agency (EPA) does not apply burn bans or regulate prescribed burning (the States do), but it monitors concentrations of both fine (< 2.5 micrometers) and coarse (between 2.5 and 10 micrometers) particles. The EPA maintains an online database of air quality levels (www.epa.gov/ebtpages/airairqunonattainment.html) that can provide valuable guidance when one is considering whether prescribed burning is an option for a particular area, including the ability to produce maps that highlight areas with chronic air quality problems. In the Southern States, a relatively small number of counties have recently been considered in nonattainment for fine particles, resulting in restrictions on prescribed burning. As of April 2005, these counties were in Alabama (Shelby and Jefferson and parts of Walker and Jackson), Georgia (all of the counties surrounding Atlanta as well as many nearby counties, and Walker and Catoosa on the Georgia-Tennessee border), North Carolina (Catawba, Davidson, and Guilford), and Virginia (counties adjacent to Washington, DC).

Fuel loads—It is important to consider what types and quantities of fuels are present when estimating the potential for achieving desired management goals through prescribed burning. For example, some forests may have accumulated so much litter or midstory vegetation that a wildfire could severely damage or kill the pine overstory. While a series of carefully planned dormant-season prescribed burns performed under moist conditions might slowly reduce fuel levels, there is the possibility that not enough fuel would be consumed to make the effort worthwhile. Rideout and others (2003) found that wet fuels produced spotty fires and consumed little fuel. In addition, hardwoods in a forest may create so much shade and moist litter that a prescribed burn is not possible. In such a case it may be necessary to remove the hardwoods mechanically or by applying herbicides before a prescribed burning program is possible.

Effects on fuel—Fire intensity is based on multiple factors, such as the spatial distribution and other characteristics of fuels, firing techniques, and weather conditions. None of these variables are constant over time or space, so the potential effect of prescribed burning on fuels will vary temporally with fuel moisture and weather at the time of the burn, and spatially depending on the pattern of fuels within a stand.

Ground fuels—Because of its high lignin content and density, duff is normally consumed through smoldering combustion rather than flaming (Miyanishi and Johnson 2002). Once the duff layer starts to smolder, it can continue to burn long after the flaming front has passed. Duff combustion can be a major source of smoke and of mortality of overstory trees if feeder roots have grown into the duff layer or duff has accumulated around the bases of trees and thermal girdling occurs. For example, Varner and others (2005) describe unexpected mortality in old longleaf pines after a wildfire, in an area where wildfire or prescribed burning had been excluded for decades. Even though there was no crown scorch, 91 percent of the trees with diameter at breast height (d.b.h.) > about 14 inches died within 2 years. Thick duff layers had accumulated around the bases of the trees and duff combustion was observed for several days. Varner and others (2005) speculate that duff combustion might have killed the trees by killing roots in the

duff, although thermal girdling or other stresses were also possibilities. For stands with well-developed duff layers, Varner and others (2005) recommend multiple low-intensity burns to gradually reduce the duff layer, which will train the overstory trees to produce roots below the duff layer. Nevertheless, a landowner must consider that these ground fires could severely damage or kill trees in the pine overstory.

Dead surface fuels—Pine needles are the fuel that is mainly responsible for carrying fire in loblolly pine forests (Johansen and others 1976), and keeping levels of pine needle litter low is important if one wants to minimize the intensity of a potential wildfire. Prescribed burning can be effective in reducing litter accumulations and keeping amounts of litter fuels low. However, repeated applications are usually necessary because of the high needle productivity of loblolly pine forests and the rapid rate of litter accumulation after burning.

The amount of dead fuel consumed by a prescribed burn depends on fuel moisture, fuelbed structure, firing techniques, and weather at the time of the burn. For example, Scholl and Waldrop (1999) found that winter burning reduced surface fuel weight by 38 to 80 percent in loblolly pine stands of different ages and structures in the upper Coastal Plain of South Carolina. Waldrop and others (2004) examined multiple pine-hardwood stands with varying soil moisture conditions that were prescribed burned and found that the fire reduced surface fuels on drier sites, but not on wetter sites. Rideout and Oswald (2002) found that surface fuel consumption during a prescribed burn in east Texas was minimal because of high fuel moisture, low wind speeds, and cool temperatures that resulted in a patchy, low-intensity burn. Sparks and others (2002) found that surface fuel consumption in shortleaf pine stands with a hardwood midstory was actually higher during the dormant season (49 percent) than in the growing season (41 percent) despite similar fuel moistures and lower Keetch-Byram Drought index (KBDI) values during the dormant season. The differences in surface fuel reduction were attributed to high relative humidity, low wind speed, greater fuel compaction, and greater prevalence of live fuels during the growing season.

Typically, consumption of dead surface fuel by a prescribed burn decreases as the size of the fuel increases. Multiple fires may be necessary to completely consume large woody debris such as logs if the site is wet enough to keep the debris cores moist (van Lear 1993). Consequently, a low-intensity prescribed burn consumes mostly 1-hour time-lag dead fuels (vegetation with a large surface-to-mass ratio, otherwise known as "fine fuels") whereas multiple fires are needed to fully consume larger fuels. In a shortleaf pine savanna restoration program in the Ouachita Mountains of Arkansas, a prescribed burn consumed 27 percent of post-thinning woody debris, with 60 percent of this amount being fuels in the 1-hour and 10-hour time-lag dead fuel classes (Liechty and others 2004). Similarly, Scholl and Waldrop (1999) found that burning consumed on average 28 percent of 1-hour time-lag dead fuels, 15 percent of 100-hour time-lag dead fuels, and 3 percent of 1,000-hour time-lag dead fuels in the Upper Coastal Plain of the Southeast.

How quickly quantities of dead surface fuels return to pre-burn levels depends on various factors including the openness of the site, the number of deciduous trees present, and the productivity of the site. Litter generally re-accumulates quickly during the first few seasons as released nutrient resources are utilized for foliage production, then slows down as resources are depleted. For example, McKee (1982), who compared dead surface and ground fuels in unburned pine-hardwood stands with such fuels in stands that were burned either annually or periodically (every 3 to 7 years), found that levels of dead surface and ground fuels were about 60 percent lower in annually burned stands than in unburned stands. Fuel levels in periodically burned stands were only 30 percent lower than fuel levels in unburned controls, which suggest that the majority of dead surface and ground fuels re-accumulate quickly. The density of trees on a site strongly affects the rate of re-accumulation. According to Johansen and others (1976), a loblolly pine stand with 70 square feet of basal area per acre would have an estimated 3.2 tons of dead surface fuels per acre 3 years after a fire while a stand with 150 square feet of basal area per acre would have 5.7 tons of such fuels per acre. If there are no further fires, equilibrium is eventually reached between decomposition and litter production.

Live surface fuels—In open loblolly pine forests, most understory plant species re-sprout vigorously following fire. Therefore, prescribed burning strategies for live fuels reduction and maintenance require repeated applications of fire and consideration of the ecological responses of multiple species. Grasses and forbs recover rapidly immediately following a burn but then decrease over time as shrubs recover and become more dominant (Johansen and others 1976). In uneven-aged loblolly pine-shortleaf pine stands in Arkansas, there was a shift in species composition from woody to herbaceous species when the interval between burns was 3 years, but not at longer intervals (Cain and others 1998). For common live surface fuels, such as sweetgum (*Liquidambar styraciflua*) and oaks, it is reasonable to expect an understory to regain its former size within 3 to 5 years.

Repeated prescribed burns can reduce live fuel loadings, but only if the fires occur frequently enough either to exhaust root reserves or to kill short-lived plants before they can produce seeds. For example, a long-term experiment at the Santee Experimental Forest in the Coastal Plain of South Carolina found that annual growing season prescribed burns converted a woody-dominated understory to a herbaceous-dominated one (Waldrop and others 1992). However, prescribed burning every 3 to 7 years was not sufficient to exhaust hardwood root reserves even after 43 years, and the understory was dominated by numerous hardwood stems and short shrubs created by re-sprouting. Periodic burning can increase the presence of herbaceous species below the hardwood understory for 1 to 2 years after each prescribed burn, but the woody species eventually regrow enough to shade out most of the herbaceous species (fig. 3). The effects of prescribed burns on live fuels are generally greater when burns are performed more frequently (every year or so) and during the growing season (White and others 1990). Growth of loblolly pine trees is not necessarily related to the reduction in competition that results from burning (Waldrop and others 1987), but because of the potential of hotter summer burns to scorch the crowns of young pines, winter burning is preferred in younger pine stands (McKevlin and McKee 1986).

Figure 3—Herbaceous species beneath a re-sprouting hardwood layer. (Photo courtesy of Douglas J. Marshall)

Season of burn is an important factor in plant community dynamics. Reduction of live surface fuels will typically be less if prescribed burning is done during the dormant season rather than during the growing season, even if the treatment is applied annually. For example, annual winter burns and annual burns during other seasons had about the same effect on hardwood cover at the Santee Experimental Forest, although the annual winter burns did increase cover of herbaceous species, especially legumes (Waldrop and others 1992). Annual winter burning for 43 years also increased the density of small (< 1 inch d.b.h.) hardwoods to more than 16,000 stems per acre, mainly because of re-sprouting of sweetgum. Therefore, it should not be assumed that a prescribed burning program will always eliminate live surface fuels and reduce overall wildfire risk.

The susceptibility of live surface fuels to topkill decreases with increasing stem diameter (Hare 1965). Larger plants tend to have thicker bark that provides more insulation, and have foliage and buds that are high enough to avoid damage. Many southern hardwoods become tolerant of most low-intensity fires once they reach a certain size. For example, Phillips and others (2004) found that the majority of stems killed by a moderate-intensity winter prescribed burn were in the 1 to 2 inch d.b.h. classes, and that mortality in larger d.b.h. classes was limited. Boyer (1990) looked at a mature longleaf pine stand with a hardwood midstory that had been previously managed with periodic dormant-season prescribed burns. Two summer burns, two years apart were applied in an effort to eliminate the hardwoods by exhausting their root reserves. Although 58 percent of hardwoods < 1.5 inches d.b.h. died, only 13 to 15 percent of hardwoods with d.b.h. from 2 to 3 inches died and only 4 to 7 percent of the 4 inch and greater d.b.h. classes died. The majority of hardwood mortality occurred after the second prescribed burn and probably resulted from exhaustion of limited root reserves in saplings.

Susceptibility to topkill also varies among species. Although many mature oaks (*Quercus* spp.) and hickories (*Carya* spp.) have relatively thick bark, species such as red maple (*Acer rubrum*), sweetgum, and American beech (*Fagus grandifolia*) have thinner bark and are presumably more likely to be girdled by fires (Harmon 1984). However, these differences may not translate directly into inter-specific variation in topkill because bark thickness increases with d.b.h. for these species. Thus, older thin-barked species may survive a fire while young saplings of thick-barked species are killed.

Ladder and crown fuels—Ladder and crown fuels are live and dead fuels that allow a fire to climb from the ground to the crown canopy, and include grasses, shrubs, and trees. For mature stands with a midstory, prescribed burning is more difficult in stands with ladder or crown fuels. The presence of such fuels in a mature stand does not mean that prescribed fire cannot be used, but it means that only low-intensity fires that will affect only the understory can be employed. One major impact of prescribed burning on overstory trees is crown scorch, which is greatest when overstory trees are young and have foliage close to the surface fuelbed. However, even severe crown scorch may have little impact on the survival of larger trees. In a 17-year-old loblolly pine plantation in South Carolina, co-dominant trees that were completely scorched suffered only 20 percent mortality, whereas intermediate trees suffered 20 to 30 percent mortality (Waldrop and van Lear 1984). No dominant trees died as a result of crown scorch. In a 19-year-old naturally regenerated loblolly pine stand in southeastern Louisiana, incidence of severe crown scorch following a winter burn was greatest in dense, lightly thinned plots that had a large number of small trees (Lilieholm and Hu 1987). Fire-induced mortality was significant only in the suppressed crown class.

Crown scorch may actually increase available fuels in the short term as the dead needles and leaves in the crown dry out and become more flammable. If the branches are not killed, the needles and leaves will fall within 2 to 3 weeks and either accumulate on the ground or be draped on the remains of understory stems, which are also drying and becoming more flammable. If the branches are killed, abscission will not occur and the leaves and needles can remain elevated for a few months if sheltered enough. Slow decomposition of dead branches as they are broken off by wind and rain will also increase fuel levels on the ground. Outcalt and Wade (2004), who examined both natural stands and plantations of slash pine that burned in the 1998 Florida wildfires, found that tree mortality was the same for stands that were prescribed burned 3 months before the wildfire and stands that had not been prescribed burned in 2 to 3 years. Outcalt and Wade (2004) suggest that scorch that occurred during prescribed burning had resulted in heavy needle drape and had given rise to a layer of dried small woody stems, and that the presence of both of these fuels in the same stands was a condition favorable for subsequent intense wildfire, with post-prescribed burning stress also playing a role in tree susceptibility. However, mortality was quite low in stands burned 1.5 years previously, and this suggests that there may be a window of decreased potential fire intensity as ground fuels are starting to decompose but before dead surface fuels have started to accumulate. Nevertheless, prescribed burning does not necessarily create fire-proofed conditions—park-like and fuel-free forests.

Application—It is imperative that persons without burning experience train with a State-certified burn manager before attempting to conduct a prescribed burn. This publication does not present instructions for prescribed burning, as prescribed burning is an established practice. Detailed instructions for conducting a burn are given in the 1989 U.S. Forest Service publication "A guide for prescribed fire in southern forests" (Wade and Lunsford 1989).

Season of prescribed burning—Most prescribed burns are conducted during the dormant season (late winter or early spring) when cool temperatures and relatively high fuel moisture limit the danger of escaped prescribed burns and damage to overstory trees. Dormant season burning can be effective in temporarily reducing fuel loads but may be less effective in eliminating established hardwoods or preventing fuel re-accumulation. It is best thought of as a means of maintaining forest structure and species composition, and as a game management tool. Repeated dormant season burns are sometimes also used to prepare an area for eventual growing season burning if fuel levels are too high, although injury or mortality of overstory pines is still possible.

Growing season burning, which takes place in mid to late spring, is primarily used for hardwood elimination and for promoting an herbaceous-dominated understory at the expense of a woody midstory. In addition, growing season prescribed burns can be used to encourage flowering in savanna species such as Carolina wiregrass (*Aristida stricta*). At the Savannah River Site in South Carolina, up to 2,500 acres of pine-hardwood forests are burned during the growing season, primarily in red-cockaded woodpecker (*Picoides borealis*) areas, and up to 3,000 acres are burned during the dormant season (Shea and Bayle 2006). Most stands are on a 3 to 5 year prescribed burn rotation, except for areas near sensitive buildings and roads where burns are spaced at least 10 years apart.

Season of burn and fire frequency are important considerations in designing programs to restore native herbaceous communities, but their relative importance is debated (Brockway and Lewis 1997, Glitzenstein and others 2003). Some land managers use growing season burns to eliminate larger hardwoods and then use dormant season burning to maintain open conditions. For example, at Kisatchie National Forest in Louisiana, about one-third of the prescribed burns occur during the growing season, although they are used for hardwood suppression and not for changing the understory species composition. In overstocked stands, growing season burns on a rotation of 2 to 3 years are used to decrease hardwood stocking to an acceptable level and then dormant season burns are used

every 3 to 5 years to maintain hardwood levels (Personal communication. 2006. Frank Yerby, District Ranger, Kisatchie National Forest, 2500 Shreveport Highway, Pineville, LA 71360).

Costs—Smidt and others (2005) found that the average cost of contracted prescribed burning in the South was $20 to $30 per acre. Costs can be as low as $10 per acre where there is little need for concern about smoke and fire escape or as high as $40 per acre where careful attention needs to be paid around residential or urban areas. Many State forestry agencies will assist with or conduct prescribed burns for small landowners for a price, and some will lend torches and other equipment. Also, most agencies will help landowners draw up prescribed burning management plans.

Mechanical Treatments

Overview—If prescribed burning is not an acceptable management option, then a mechanical treatment may be effective in reducing wildfire risk by redistributing the fuels closer to the ground, creating a more compact fuel bed. There are two general types of mechanical treatments: those that rearrange biomass and leave it on a site, and those that remove biomass from a site. The application of mechanical techniques to fuels management in the South is challenging for three reasons. First, southern forests have rapid vegetation growth rates and a large number of hardwood species that vigorously re-sprout after mechanical treatment. Thus, if the hardwoods are only cut and not killed, it may only take a few years for them to regain their previous size and negate any wildfire risk reduction benefit. Second, wet soils and seasonal wetlands can limit the use of heavy equipment for extended periods during the year. And third, mechanical treatments are relatively expensive compared to prescribed burning.

With the creation of the Healthy Forests Initiative in the early 2000s, one-time funding for mechanical operations became available to public agencies, and this type of treatment increased substantially. On Federal lands in the South, the area of land treated by mechanical methods has risen to over 150,000 acres per year (U.S. Department of the Interior 2006b). However, the area of Federal land that was prescription burned annually in the South averaged more than 1 million acres during 2003 to 2005, and the vast majority of the mechanical operations appear to have been one-time treatments for reducing excessive fuel loads prior to burning.

Types of mechanical treatments—Land management agencies have experimented with many types of mechanical fuel treatments, ranging from use of machines that gather small stems and branches and form them into bundles for collection (Rummer and others 2004) to use of cut-to-length harvesters that provide stems for small chippers (Bolding and Lanford 2005). Many of these treatments have been found to be unrealistically expensive or time-consuming and have limited applicability for wildland fuels treatments in the South. However, cost figures may change if markets for biomass for energy production continue to develop. It appears that mulching (mastication) and chipping, both of which are normally used as one-time precursors to prescribed burning, are the only mechanical treatments now in common use in the South. The infrequency of use of mechanical treatments is based on hardwood re-sprouting rates and treatment costs rather than a lack of information. Both mulching and chipping operations produce chips, but mulching operations leave the chips in the forest while chipping operations remove the chips. A mulching operation is considered pre-commercial, whereas a chipping operation could be considered pre-commercial, commercial, or a combination of the two depending on how costs are absorbed and the types of chips produced (pulp quality or furnace quality).

Pre-commercial versus commercial operations—In traditional forestry, a pre-commercial operation is one in which understory or midstory stems are cut and either left onsite or removed, and the operation generally loses money but leads to increased future profits by encouraging the remaining trees to grow faster. In contrast, a commercial operation removes stems from the midstory or overstory and a profit is generally made. However, in modern forestry, the difference between the two terms is less clear due to increased use of logging slash and small stems for furnace chips (fig. 4), and because multiple wood products may be generated during harvests (e.g., chips, pulpwood, and sawtimber). While most examples of mechanical fuel management in loblolly pine forests would be considered pre-commercial operations, the immediate expenditures have to be balanced with the benefit of reduced wildfire risk and the increase in the future value of crop trees (Mason and others 2006).

A money-losing pre-commercial chipping operation (removing a dense understory of small stems) could be performed immediately before a profitable operation (thinning of overstory) to improve access and reduce the

Figure 4—A commercial chipper used for producing furnace fuel. (Photo courtesy of Douglas J. Marshall)

risk of post-harvest wildfire. Some federal cost-share programs, such as the Stewardship Incentives Program and the Forestry Incentives Program (although both of these were de-authorized in 2002), may recommend thinning of pine stands, but market conditions determine the commercial aspect of the operation.

Crush and chop—Although not very common, the crush and chop treatment is occasionally used for fuel reduction. This method is the most basic mechanical treatment, in which weight alone is used to reposition fuels close to the ground. It is normally used in the South during site preparation to kill hardwoods, to prepare an area for prescribed burning, and to facilitate planting. A common form of this method is roller-drum chopping (fig. 5), in which a tractor pulls a water-filled, ribbed metal drum across a site. In overstocked young pine stands where hand thinning is impractical due to the large number of stems, roller-chopping has been used as a low-cost pre-commercial thinning alternative that also reduces insect susceptibility and wildfire hazard, and promotes growth of the residual trees. However, for fuel management purposes, the technique is crude and useful only in stands where the target trees are small (e.g., < 5 inches d.b.h.) and can be pushed over, and where the machine can travel in relatively straight

Figure 5—A roller-drum chopper. (Photo courtesy of David J. Moorhead/Forestry Images)

lines. Moreover, given the width of the chopped rows (10+ feet) and the limited ability of the remaining young trees to close the canopy, there is a strong possibility that hardwoods or other woody species will quickly establish themselves in the rows and negate any fuel reduction benefit. For these reasons, the crush and chop treatment has limited applicability in fuel management.

Mulching—Unlike the crush and chop treatment, a mulching operation is intended to break fuels into small pieces. Windell and Bradshaw (2000) classified mulching equipment as either vertical-shaft (traditional mowers) or horizontal-shaft (mulchers that grid downward). These can be mounted on equipment ranging from small rubber-tracked machines with 90 to 100 horsepower (HP) grinding attachments (fig. 6) to large machines with 400 HP grinders (fig. 7). Heavy-duty mowers are useful when fuels are small enough to be pushed over. However, for sites with an established woody midstory, machines with front-based cutters will probably be needed.

At Fort Jackson, SC, a mulching operation in 2006 was used to treat a pine-dominated understory and midstory and keep the fuels low enough to the ground (< 36 inches) to allow ATV travel during a subsequent prescribed burn (fig. 8). In that operation a highly maneuverable rubber-tracked loader (ASV PosiTrack™ RC-100) with a 100-HP mulching head (Fecon 100 HP) was used more as a mower than as a mulcher, as the stems were just cut and not ground up. Since the machine was not used to mulch and cut, the crew had a high productivity rate (about 7 acres per day). A mulching operation at Bankhead National Forest in Alabama in 2005 used a mulching head on a skidder (fig. 9) in a similar way. Both operations produced a fuel bed of severed stems rather than chips. In contrast, an operation at Conecuh National Forest in 2005 to 2006 employed a crawler with a Fecon RT 400 mulching head (fig. 10) to grind fuels into chips and incorporate them into the top 3 inches of soil (fig. 11) to reduce the intensity of a subsequent prescribed burn. This produced a cleaner site, but at a low rate of productivity (about 1 acre per day).

Chipping—Although mulching is more commonly used for fuel management, chipping is becoming increasingly important in the South. The increasing popularity of chips for the energy market is a major factor. Many pulp mills have their own wood-based power plants in order to minimize waste and decrease overall costs. These plants are often connected to regional power grids, and mills may sell their excess power to power companies. When oil prices are low, the energy-producing parts of these mills are often underutilized. However, oil prices started rising in 2005 and demand for furnace (dirty) chips for energy production has

Figure 6—ASV PosiTrack RC-100 with Fecon 87-HP mulching head. (Photo courtesy of Douglas J. Marshall)

Figure 7—Fecon RT-400 with 400-HP mulching head. (Photo courtesy of Douglas J. Marshall)

Figure 8—Mechanical operation at Fort Jackson, SC. (Photo courtesy of Douglas J. Marshall)

Figure 10—An intense mulching operation at Conecuh National Forest in Alabama with a Fecon RT-400. (U.S. Forest Service photo)

Figure 9—Mechanical mulching operation on the Bankhead National Forest in Alabama. (U.S. Forest Service photo)

Figure 11—Fuelbed of chips incorporated into the soil by a Fecon RT-400 at Conecuh National Forest in Alabama. (Photo courtesy of Douglas J. Marshall)

been rising in response. However, while rising oil prices may increase the demand for wood chips, the accompanying rise in diesel prices limits the distance chips can be hauled.

Feasibility—For most southern operations, the main fuel targets for mechanical treatments will be the midstory and understory vegetation, although selective thinning of the overstory is also a possibility. Many mechanical operations are precursors for a subsequent prescribed burning program. Therefore, the feasibility of a subsequent prescribed burning program should also be evaluated. Offsite problems that can result from mechanical operations are less serious than those that can result from prescribed burning, so cost, access, and productivity are the most important considerations. It may be possible to combine mechanical operations with prescribed burning in ways that increase cost-effectiveness.

Roads—As in the case of prescribed burning, the road system should be evaluated; it should not be assumed that the existence of a paved road network means that it will be possible to get heavy equipment to a site. Three easily overlooked but important questions are whether the roads have turns that are too sharp to be negotiated by large flatbed trucks, how much weight the bridges can handle, and whether it will be possible to unload equipment at the worksite without causing traffic problems. Stanturf and others (2003b) recognized the limitations road networks place on heavy equipment use in the wildland-urban interface and recommended the use of small, maneuverable machines that can be unloaded and used in tight quarters. However, small equipment are limited in horsepower, and this means that there is a practical limit to what size vegetation can be treated and how quickly. For example, a 100-HP mulching head used at Conecuh National Forest in Alabama could not efficiently cut down large midstory trees (> 6 inches d.b.h.). It also took the machine a long time to mulch large stems once they were on the ground (fig. 12). Similar problems were encountered when underpowered equipment was used to mulch large logs at Jones State Forest in Texas (fig. 13).

Soils—Soil type can largely determine whether mechanical operations are feasible and what type of equipment should be used. Rutting is a concern in wet conditions where soils are fine and clayey, while compaction can become a major problem with multiple machine passes over the same area. Tracked machines distribute their weight more evenly than do wheeled vehicles, but they turn by swiveling, and this can damage the roots and boles of residual trees. The use of smaller and lighter machines reduces these concerns, and these machines can operate in wetter soil conditions with higher utilization rates. State-level best management

Figure 12—Incomplete mulching at Conecuh National Forest in Alabama. (Photo courtesy of Douglas J. Marshall)

Figure 13—Incomplete mulching at Jones State Forest in Texas. (Photo courtesy of Douglas J. Marshall)

practices (BMPs) for timber harvesting operations may apply in many mechanical treatment operations.

Slopes—If large parts of the terrain exceed 30 percent slope, then mechanical treatment may not be a realistic option. The Georgia forestry BMP guide recommends that harvesting be limited to slopes under 40 percent, and mechanical site preparation be limited to slopes under 30 percent (Georgia Forestry Commission 1999). Similarly, the Alabama BMP guide suggests 25 percent as the maximum slope for site preparation and recommends that logging on steep slopes is kept to short stretches (Alabama Forestry Commission 1999). During a mulching operation at Fort Benning, Georgia, a wheeled machine with a mulching head mounted on it had trouble maneuvering on clayey soils with 15 percent or greater slopes, and had to be replaced with a more expensive tracked machine (Rummer and others 2006).

Target fuels—The most likely target vegetation is a woody midstory characterized by many small stems and limited visibility. In areas with well- to excessively drained sandy soils such as Fort Jackson, SC, the midstory will probably be dominated by volunteer pines and scrub oaks. As soil moisture increases, the woody component will become more dominated by hardwoods and shrubs. For mechanical operations to be successful, the target vegetation must be large enough and rigid enough to be susceptible to cutting.

The density of residual trees must be evaluated with an eye to controlling damage caused by heavy equipment. If there are too many residual trees, a machine may not be able to move effectively or quickly through a site. In addition, if stand visibility from inside a cab is limited, this may result in excessive damage to residual trees, or productivity may decline.

The composition of the fuels being treated also affects the type of product that can be produced. Chippers that are designed to produce clean (pulp quality) chips are designed to process softwoods (mainly conifers). Some hardwoods, such as sweetgum, can be chipped without much difficulty, but others, such as oaks, are too hard to be chipped without increased wear to chipper teeth. Therefore, the softwood-hardwood ratio of target trees strongly affects the economics of a chipping operation. Different types of chippers are suitable for use in different kinds of fuel management operations. Small chippers similar to those used by arboriculturists, which produce a mixture of leaves and chips, are effective in operations where small stems are being collected by hand. This type of equipment is designed for limited use with small diameter material and is not suited for continuous use with whole trees. For commercial operations where larger stems (2 to 3 inches d.b.h.) are

being chipped, a more rugged piece of equipment is needed. Some commercial chippers can delimb and debark trees of some species, but this type of equipment is very expensive and difficult to move around, which limits its use in pre-commercial operations.

Available markets for chips or small-diameter stems—A market for small-diameter stems is a function of the cost to get the material from the forest to the purchaser as well as the ability of the purchaser to absorb material. For a chipping operation to be feasible, a realistic economic analysis of local markets is needed. Since most coal power plants require pulverized fuels, woody fuels are typically limited to 2 percent (fuels blended before injection into the furnace) or 10 percent (fuels injected separately) (Hughes 2000). Therefore, there may be a limit to the amount of chips a plant will accept.

Effects on fuels—Since some mechanical operations in the South will be used as precursors to prescribed burning, their effects on fuels should be considered.

Ground fuels—If large stems are dragged through the forest, the duff layer can be scraped from the center of the skid trails and deposited along the sides. For example, on relatively dry sites in a Piedmont pine-hardwood forest, thinning operations reduced the duff and litter layers only in localized areas (Waldrop and others 2004). Otherwise, significant effects to the ground fuels should not be expected unless mulching is done, soils are wet, or rutting occurs.

Dead surface fuels—In mulching operations, the main goal is to convert live fuels into pieces 1 to 5 inches long and reposition them close to the ground. Thus, mulching typically increases loadings of dead surface fuels while reducing loadings of live fuels. Larger dead fuels get treated as well because the process is non-selective. Rummer and others (2006) found that a hammer flail machine and a fixed-tooth machine produced mulch in different mixtures of sizes in an operation at Fort Benning in Georgia. The hammer flail machine produced a smaller proportion of mulch under 0.25 inch (1-hour time-lag dead fuels) (25 percent versus 38 percent). The two machines produced about the same proportion of 0.25 to 1.0 inch mulch (10-hour time-lag dead fuels) (47 percent). The fixed tooth machine produced a smaller proportion of 1- to 3-inch mulch (100-hour time-lag dead fuels) (15 percent versus 28 percent). If the mulch that is produced in a fuel reduction operation consists mostly of smaller material, as it did at Fort Benning, it should burn readily when fuel moisture is low. Also, it is usually expected that fuels in these size classes will form a compacted fuelbed, and that this will result in reduced fire intensities. However, the fuels produced by mulching do not compact completely, as they are irregularly shaped and almost strip-like (fig. 14).

Interactions among topography, equipment selection, and impact intensity affect the production of dead surface fuels in mechanical operations, especially in areas where trees are processed. For example, dead fine fuels (1- to 100-hour size classes) increased in dry and intermediate areas after a thinning operation (Waldrop and others 2004). Discarded crowns were a major source of the increase in these fuels. There was no increase in fine or large fuels in wet areas, possibly because harvesting was limited in wet areas or because the trees were being delimbed in drier locations.

Live surface fuels—Live surface fuels are the main targets of a mechanical operation, and are often in the form of a thick shrub layer that can result in high fire intensities during a prescribed burn. When this layer is dominated by woody species that can re-sprout and grow quickly (e.g., sweetgum and yaupon (*Ilex vomitoria*), as is usually the case, any reduction in live surface fuels that results from a mechanical operation will be temporary.

Because there is no selectivity, a mulching treatment would be expected to reduce all live surface fuels that are accessible to the cutting head. Inaccessible fuels could be pockets of material protected by residual trees (fig. 15) or in wet areas susceptible to rutting or compaction. Mulched fuels are left on site, but are usually not thick enough to prevent re-sprouting or seed germination. A chipping operation removes stems more selectively. If chips are being harvested for pulp, pines and some hardwoods (often sweetgum) may be utilized, while other hardwoods may be avoided. Furthermore, since tree stems are usually brought to the chipper with a skidder, the stems must be big enough to be grabbed and large enough to be chipped (usually a minimum d.b.h. of 3 to 5 inches). The travel of heavy equipment in a chipping operation can also reduce small live fuels by crushing them. Phillips and others (2004) found that a thinning from below in a Coastal Plain pine-hardwood forest reduced average stem density from 5,075 to 3,725 stems per acre, with the bulk of the reduction in the ≤ 2-inch d.b.h. class.

Ladder and crown fuels—Vegetation can be thinned or pruned to disrupt the distribution of live and dead vegetation

Figure 14—A mulched fuel bed at Jones State Forest in Texas. (Photo courtesy of Douglas J. Marshall)

Figure 15—Mulched area at Jones State Forest in Texas with minor fuel pockets. (Photo courtesy of Douglas J. Marshall)

from the ground to the canopy of a stand, so that a fire will not be able to climb into the canopy. Pruning operations are usually performed by hand crews that trim the branches of trees up to 8 or 16 feet above the ground (to the height of one-half or one log). Pruning operations are currently relatively uncommon in loblolly pine stands in the South, but remain a viable option for mechanical treatment of trees. Thinning operations target trees that are suppressed, overtopped, or diseased, as well as healthy dominant and co-dominant trees in the overstory where stand density is a concern. Normal commercial harvesting equipment such as skidders and feller-bunchers can be used to harvest larger trees; small machines with low-horsepower mulching heads can maneuver around larger trees but cannot fell them. Chainsaws can be used to fell small or large ladder fuels. Thinning operations can be commercial (where most of the trees that are cut down are delivered to a mill) or pre-commercial (where the thinned trees are redistributed on a site, and become surface fuels). Note that large amounts of slash may be left on the site even in a commercial thinning.

Application—If a mechanical treatment is to be followed with a prescribed burn, it is important to schedule the burn

at the proper time. If the site is burned during winter to minimize fire intensity associated with dead fuels, there will be little impact on re-sprouting woody species. On the other hand, if the prescribed burn is performed soon after spring starts and leaves are being produced, the number of re-sprouting woody species will be reduced. However, if the sprouts are given too much time for growth, the site may produce too many live fuels to be treated effectively at fuel moisture levels suitable for prescribed burning. For example, after a mulching operation at Fort Benning, Georgia, in October (early fall), researchers burned mulched areas either in late winter (4 months post-treatment), spring (7 months post-treatment), or summer (10 months post-treatment) (Rummer and others 2006). The winter and spring burns effectively reduced re-sprouting, but the summer burn was effective only on dry sites. On most of the bottomland sites, the rapid sprouting produced so much live fuel that the burn was uneven and the researchers felt that the window of opportunity for fuel reduction had passed.

Costs—For commercial operations like chipping and thinning, profitability is based largely on pulpwood prices and diesel fuel costs, both of which have been highly variable over the last few years (2005 to 2007). For non-commercial operations, the high cost of heavy equipment makes it likely that most mechanical fuel reduction treatments will be performed by private contractors who will either bid for contracts or provide site-specific estimates. Unfortunately, since mechanical fuel reduction treatments are a relatively new activity in the South, contractors and customers have few guidelines for estimating costs. Any operation involves multiple financial variables such as fuel type and density, tract size, equipment choice, and restrictions intended to minimize site damage. Therefore, it is not practical to estimate the costs of specific fuel reduction treatments in this publication. Instead, anecdotal information from recent operations is used to establish a range of possible prices. Acceptable cost levels may vary considerably, and depend on anticipated land use following the treatment (i.e., forestry, development, etc.).

Mulching—For several recent mulching operations in the Southern United States, costs were highly variable ($200 to $650 per acre), and most operations were underbid. One of the biggest reasons for underbidding was overestimation by contractors of expected productivity rates. Contractors usually pay their crews on an hourly basis, whereas contracts are made on an area basis, so delays in production can quickly lead to loss of profitability. These delays can be caused by equipment failure (e.g., grinding teeth breaking), terrain conditions, or other restrictions—such as being allowed to work in wildland-urban interface areas only during daylight hours. One unexpected source of delays may be over-treatment of fuels by contractors who are skilled at preparing areas for housing developments or agricultural operations. In a recent mulching operation at Fort Benning, Georgia, a wheeled mulching machine was used initially. However, this machine could not climb steep slopes (> 35 percent) and got stuck in soft soils, so a more expensive tracked machine was brought in to finish the job. The wheeled machine cost about $258 per acre; the tracked machine cost about $171 per acre in flat areas and up to about $650 per acre in the steep areas (Rummer and others 2006).

Chipping—Chipping operations have been promoted as a way to reduce wildfire hazard by removing pre-commercial fuels (Bolding and Lanford 2005), but limited recent experience in the South suggests that such operations are not economically attractive under present conditions. Since chipping for fuel management is assumed to be based on the contractor selling the chips (versus leaving them on the site), the economics of the chip market and operating costs very largely determine the feasibility of an operation. The current (2006) economic conditions in the South do not promote pre-commercial chipping. Starting in the late 1990s, the price of pine pulpwood declined drastically because of

overproduction of trees and excess mill capacity (Harris and others 2005), and the cost of diesel fuel has continued to increase. As a consequence, it is becoming increasing difficult to sell pre-commercial thinning chips. Opportunistic chipping of branches and tops during a commercial harvest may still be profitable, however.

Bolding and Lanford (2005) described a cut-to-length thinning operation that harvested both commercial (4+ inches d.b.h.) and pre-commercial (0.5 to 4 inches d.b.h.) stems. A harvester (Timbco T-415C) delimbed the commercial stems and then cut them into 20- foot lengths. Pre-commercial stems were cut and piled separately. A forwarder (Fabtek 546B) then collected the stems and transported them to a loading deck, where commercial stems were loaded into trucks and pre-commercial stems were loaded into a small chipper (Bandit 1850) that fed the chips into a waiting trailer. One major limitation was that the chipper could not operate as fast as it was receiving stems from the forwarder. Recent pre-commercial chipping operations at Kisatchie National Forest during 2003 to 2005 cost only $2 to $5 per acre for the actual operation and $15 to $18 per acre when administrative costs were considered. Since the operations were part of a midstory and understory removal, both clean (pulp quality) and dirty (boiler quality) chips were produced.

Minimum treatment area is central to the subject of treatment costs. If contractors will be used for an operation, then the minimum treatment area and expected travel times within the area must be taken into account when designing a request for bids. For example, at Fort Jackson, South Carolina, it was determined that about 1,000 cords of wood in a localized area would be needed for a treatment to be commercially viable (Personal communication. 2006. John Maitland, Forestry Team Leader, Directorate of Logistics and Engineering, Building 2563, Essayons Way, Fort Jackson, SC 29207).

Herbicide Treatments

Overview—Herbicides are one alternative for hazardous fuel treatment in the South, particularly for controlling invasive species of plants. However, research on the use of forestry herbicides usually focuses on site preparation and release operations during the first 10 years of stand establishment. Hence, apart from a few studies of midstory tree removal in degraded longleaf pine stands, there has been little scientific research in the area of herbicide use for fuel management later in the life of stands. Finally, understory and midstory hazardous fuels in loblolly pine forests tend to be dense and not readily susceptible to herbicide treatment.

To remove unwanted vegetation below a loblolly pine canopy without harming the overstory pines would require a ground application targeting specific plants.

Nevertheless, the use of herbicides to manage hazardous fuel may be a realistic option in certain situations. For example, if the midstory vegetation has become so large that a prescribed burn would have little effect, an herbicide application can remove it with minimal impact on overstory loblolly pine. Provencher and others (2001) found that a herbicide-prescribed burning treatment was far more effective at removing larger oaks than prescribed burning alone. Although herbicides cannot replace prescribed burning or mechanical operations in cases where dead fuels must be removed or repositioned closer to the ground, they are useful as preliminary treatments to kill or suppress live fuels. Herbicides can also be useful as a followup treatment to kill re-sprouting woody species after a prescribed burn or mechanical operation, especially if the goal is to promote an herbaceous-dominated understory.

This section is not intended to show how to apply herbicides, but to provide enough information so that landowners can judge whether herbicides are a realistic option for hazardous fuel reduction. Forestry herbicides can cause offsite damage if applied improperly and may contain additives that can cause health problems. For these reasons, users must have licenses to purchase and apply many full-strength herbicides. Some herbicides can be bought without permits, but it is recommended that only trained personnel apply the herbicides, since misapplication can result in damage to the loblolly pine overstory, or other onsite and offsite problems.

Feasibility—The effectiveness of herbicide treatments intended to reduce fuels depends on the existing vegetation, topography, and other local restrictions. There are three situations in which it may be practical to use herbicides for fuel management:

1. Woody understory vegetation is targeted for removal, and the overstory is able to respond to released resources and fill in canopy openings after an herbicide treatment. The overstory trees must have healthy crowns (at least one-third of total height) and be able to respond to the release. In this scenario, competition with overstory trees is expected to limit the growth of re-sprouting vegetation in the understory.

2. Woody understory vegetation is targeted for removal but the overstory canopy is not dense enough to shade out re-sprouting vegetation after a herbicide treatment. Repeated follow-up treatments (mechanical or prescribed burning treatments) at regular intervals may be needed to slow

natural vegetation succession and to maintain low levels of forest fuels.

3. Invasive, exotic plant species are targeted for removal, and herbicides are the only effective treatment.

Terrain—Topography affects herbicide treatments by limiting the type of equipment that can be effectively used. For example, on slopes > 20 to 30 percent, efficient and nondestructive ground application may be limited, particularly if the potential for herbicides to move during heavy rainfall events is high. Although steep areas can be bypassed during treatment, this may result in high fuel zones that may negate any long-term benefits of a fuel reduction program.

Soils—Sandy soils that drain water quickly can limit the effectiveness of soil-active herbicides. If there is too little rain, herbicide movement toward the roots of the targeted plant species may be limited. Conversely, too much rain will cause herbicides to quickly leach out of the upper layers of soil. In contrast, clayey and loamy soils can quickly immobilize soil-active herbicide. Where this is a problem, soil application should be avoided or the application rate should be increased.

Target vegetation—The size of the target vegetation in a fuel reduction treatment can be a good indicator of the potential effectiveness of herbicides. It usually takes more herbicide to kill larger plants. Wilkins and others (1993b) found that oaks > 6 inches d.b.h. were unaffected by soil active hexazinone. Similarly, Nelson and others (2006) found that basal application of either imazapyr or triclopyr decreased in effectiveness as white oak (*Quercus alba*) d.b.h. increased, but that this was not the case with green ash (*Fraxinus pennsylvanica*), black cherry (*Prunus serotina*), flowering dogwood (*Cornus florida*), or red oaks (*Quercus* section *Lobatae*). According to Jones and Chamberlain (2004), broadcast applications of imazapyr and imazapyr+glyphosate had no effect on hard-mast producing species (e.g., oaks) that were > 4 inches d.b.h.

Some hardwood and woody species are not affected by certain forestry herbicides and this can limit the effectiveness of fuel reduction treatments. For example, elms (*Ulmus* spp.) are not affected by imazapyr, while sassafras (*Sassafras albidum*) is not affected by hexazinone. Similarly, Nelson and others (2006) found, in South Carolina pine-hardwood stands where stems 1 to 4 inches d.b.h. received a basal (ground-level) herbicide treatment, that imazapyr alone killed 87 percent of waxmyrtle (*Morella cerifera*) and 31 percent of sweetgum, while triclopyr alone killed 100 percent of both species. Many fire-dependent herbaceous species such as wiregrass are tolerant of imazapyr (Litt and others 2001). Even a non-selective herbicide such as triclopyr, which controls most hardwoods, has little effect on grasses. In addition, some herbicides cannot be mixed together, or may be less effective in combination than if applied alone. Therefore, mixing herbicides for specific target vegetation is not always possible.

Effects on fuel—Since herbicides can take several weeks to kill live vegetation, the effects of a treatment will not be seen immediately. If live trees are the target vegetation, leaves or needles will fall within a few months, followed by branches over the next 1 to 2 years. It may require several years for large stems to decay sufficiently to begin breaking up and falling. Dead fuels killed by herbicides may increase the susceptibility of an area to a severe wildfire for some period of time until decay of the fuels begins (Brose and Wade 2002).

Ground fuels—Because herbicides are designed to affect plant metabolic processes, their direct effects on decomposition and duff are usually limited. For example, Fletcher and Freedman (1986) found that while high concentrations of some herbicides decreased decomposition rates in the forest floor due to toxicity, the thresholds were at least 50 times normal forestry application levels. However, an herbicide application during the growing season will add significantly to the litter layer once the leaves or needles of the targeted vegetation begin to fall. Further, presence of a dense shrub layer, even if the layer is killed by the herbicide, may collect leaves and become a ladder fuel. If these conditions coincide with the wildfire season, the hazardous fuel condition may be significantly worsened (Outcalt and Wade 2004).

Dead surface fuels—The production of dead surface fuels as a result of an herbicide treatment is a gradual process that begins as leaves and branches begin falling and stems start to fragment and collapse. For example, Brose and Wade (2002) found that triclopyr killed a heavy gallberry (*Ilex glabra*) understory in a 17-year-old slash pine plantation, but that the dead surface fuels remained upright for 2 years and became needle-draped. Thus, there was a time lag before wildfire hazard decreased. In contrast, in a mature longleaf pine forest that had been prescription burned for over 60 years, an application of hexazinone killed 70 percent of the hardwood midstory, while prescribed burning alone removed only 2 percent (Gagnon and Jack 2004). However, without a subsequent prescribed burn there was an increase in woody debris after the herbicide treatment, and this additional debris most likely derived from the dead branches of the herbicide-treated midstory vegetation. Gagnon and Jack

(2004) suggest that an herbicide-alone management regime would eventually create high levels of forest fuels.

Live surface fuels—Since most forestry herbicides are applied at rates less than the recommended maximum (Shepard and others 2004), complete elimination of the understory vegetation is unlikely. Furthermore, since no forestry herbicide kills all plant species, and effects vary based on the vigor of plants, soil conditions, and amount of herbicide applied, some vegetation usually survives. Often, depending on the herbicide used, there is only partial topkill of a plant or partial removal of the plant's root stock, and vigorous re-sprouting may occur. For example, Boyd and others (1995) examined the long-term effects of an herbicide release operation in a loblolly pine plantation. Seven years after treatment with hexazinone, glyphosate, or imazapyr herbicide, hardwood basal area in treated plots did not differ from that in untreated plots.

Depending on the herbicide used, some understory vegetation may not be affected, and quickly expand once their competitors are removed. For example, in a Central Florida sandhill site with a heavy oak midstory, hexazinone released grasses (including wiregrass) and saw palmetto while eliminating oaks < 6 inches d.b.h. The herbicide treatment was intended to prepare the area for regular prescribed burning, and it was expected that burning would subsequently control the highly flammable saw palmetto.

Ladder and crown fuels—If sufficient herbicide is used, the midstory vegetation will die quickly, although the leaves or needles will remain attached because no abscission layer between them and the stems will be formed. This can result in a temporary increase in flammable ladder fuels.

Application—For hazardous fuel management, herbicides are most useful as a one-time application to eliminate or suppress midstory vegetation that has grown too large to be killed or suppressed by a prescribed burn. If the objective is to kill or suppress midstory vegetation that has grown too large for prescribed burning, then stem injection (fig. 16) is probably the most effective treatment. On the other hand, if the midstory vegetation is composed of numerous small stems, then a backpack-based broadcast application (fig. 17) or basal bark application may be the most cost-effective methods. If prescribed burning is an option, then spraying the re-sprouting vegetation after a prescribed burn may be more effective than burning alone (Mitchell and others 2005).

Costs—The cost of a particular herbicide application depends on the amount of acreage to be treated, the mode of

Figure 16—A tool used for stem injection. (Photo courtesy of John D. Hodges/Forestry Images)

Figure 17—Backpack application of herbicide in thick conditions. (Photo courtesy of James H. Miller/Forestry Images)

application (e.g., broadcast spray versus stem injection), and the type and amount of herbicide used. Since these factors are variable, it is not feasible to provide a general estimate of the cost of herbicide fuel reduction treatments. Smidt and others (2005) estimated that aerial mid-rotation release of pine plantations averaged about $65 per acre during 2004. Tyler and Pongetti (2006) estimated the cost of herbicide used in early and mid-rotation herbicide applications at $60 to $105 per acre. As a general rule, cost per acre will be highest for manual application of individual-tree treatments such as stem injection, due to labor costs, and lowest for aerial applications. For small tracts, however, total cost may be lower for manual applications than for mechanized or aerial applications, which may have high equipment move-in costs.

Biological Treatments

Overview—The use of livestock to suppress hazardous fuels has a long history in the United States. Because cattle grazing was an established practice with important economic consequences for local communities, natural resource managers decided to use increased cattle densities to suppress fine fuels like grasses, and this had the incidental effect that cattle broke up small slash by trampling (Zimmerman and Neuenschwander 1983). With wildfires reduced in size and intensity, pine seedlings could be released and forests could rapidly increase in tree density. This can come, however, with an accompanying increase in live and dead surface fuels, as well as ladder fuels, depending on the vegetation consumed by livestock.

According to Campbell (1948), about three-fourths of the shortleaf-loblolly pine-hardwoods forest type in the mid-central South was grazed in the mid-1900s, with 15 to 35 acres needed per cow, due to dense tree stocking and limited herbaceous vegetation. For southern forests in general, Campbell (1948) estimated that native forage only provided sufficient food for one-half the year. Most native grasses are warm-season species that die or become dormant during the winter, so there was little forage for livestock during the winter months. While livestock grazing in southern forests is not used extensively for fuel reduction purposes today, it can potentially be used to reduce certain types of live fuels. For example, sheep grazing has been used extensively in Florida to control saw palmetto. While many farmers allow their animals to roam forests for food, poor forage quality of native plants may limit the practice.

In the modern South, livestock grazing in loblolly pine stands is limited either to the first few years of stand establishment or to low-density forests that are burned regularly (Schultz 1997). State agencies have promoted silvopastoral systems as a way for landowners to increase their revenues (e.g., Husak and Grado 2002), and these systems are based on rows of trees separated by exotic pasture grasses that are regularly prescribed burned or mowed. Because livestock prefer grasses and forbs grown in open conditions, these systems are somewhat impractical for loblolly pine production. Although the use of livestock in greenbelts (herbaceous dominated strips designed to slow a wildfire) is a possibility, this does not solve the fuel management problem in the adjacent forests.

Feasibility—The effective use of livestock for fuel management in loblolly pine forests is based on saturating an area with enough livestock so that they are forced to consume less-palatable vegetation. One drawback is that livestock forced to eat low-nutrition forage may not gain the weight expected by landowners. Although livestock could be kept in an enclosed forest permanently, they would probably need supplemental feeding areas or adjacent pastures in order to gain weight as expected. Moreover, the root systems of the browsed plants may be damaged, but if they are not killed, re-sprouting plants will regain their former size within a few years.

Effects on fuel—Since livestock seek out the most nutritious food and tend to avoid dense vegetation where travel and escape is hindered, their impacts on fuels will be uneven in terms of both location and vegetation consumed. Tsiouvaras and others (1989) reported that the intensive use of goats in a Monterey pine (*Pinus radiata*)-red gum (*Eucalyptus camaldulensis*) forest in California reduced understory and midstory cover by 41 to 48 percent. Furthermore, through trampling, the goats reduced 1- and 10-hour time-lag dead fuels by 33 percent and 58 percent and the litter layer by 27 percent. However, it is important to bear in mind that this one-day study used 600 goats within an enclosed 1-ha plot, or 242 goats per acre. In addition, the goats did not kill most of the plants, and the live fuels re-accumulated within a year.

Ground fuels—Livestock do not consume ground fuels (duff), although their movement could compact these types of fuels in the trails they create.

Dead surface fuels—Livestock do not consume dead fuels unless preferred live forage is unavailable. Thill and Martin (1979) found that cattle in a fenced-in forest in Louisiana consumed dead leaves only during fall and winter, when it constituted 11 percent of their diet. However, this consumption was likely due to poor diet rather than the nutritional value of dead leaves. Since livestock prefer to avoid areas with heavy slash, their impact on large dead surface fuels will be limited. Trampling can break up smaller dead surface fuels, but it may also cause erosion and soil compaction.

Live surface fuels—As a general rule, livestock consume herbaceous plants first, followed by woody plants with limited chemical defenses in their leaves (e.g., sweetgum). Livestock consume leaves with strong chemical defenses (e.g., pines) only when other vegetation is not available. In a Louisiana study, cattle consumed the leaves of water oak (*Quercus nigra*) only during fall and early spring, when it accounted for about 6 percent of their diet (Thill and Martin 1979). During the winter, waxmyrtle and deerberry (*Vaccinium stamineum*) made up 17 percent and 7 percent of the diet, respectively. Both of these species have rigid waxy leaves and likely low nutritional value. The loss of weight in forest-browsing cattle during winter is well-known, even in open forests (Campbell 1948).

Livestock cannot be used to control the invasive cogongrass (*Imperata cylindrica*) as its leaves are high in silica and have saw-like edges (Faircloth and others 2006). Sheep and goats have been used to control saw palmetto, although it may have little dietary value, but saw palmetto leaves are too tough to be eaten by cattle (Bennett and Hicklin 1998).

Ladder and crown fuels—Even though livestock will consume the leaves of certain vines, e.g., Carolina jessamine (*Gelsemium sempervirens*), vines normally do not form a major fire hazard in loblolly pine forests. Livestock can disrupt the ladder of vegetation only from ground level to a height of about 5 feet.

Application—Livestock grazing can be used as a solution to certain fuel reduction problems when landowners have both timber and livestock-related objectives. There will likely be a tradeoff among the objectives, given the low nutritional value of some forest vegetation and the trampling damage to soils and regenerating trees.

Costs—The use of livestock to manage hazardous fuel in forests is not currently a common practice in the South, so treatment costs are unavailable. Based on western operations, the expected main cost sources would be livestock transportation, the fencing system required, and maintenance of watering areas.

Fuel Treatments Impacts and Mitigation

The previous section discussed the factors that influence the feasibility of each type of treatment, with an emphasis on operational constraints and treatment effects on fuels. In this section, the impacts of fuel treatments on a number of social and ecological values such as water quality and wildlife will be discussed. For some negative impacts, mitigation techniques are available (e.g., re-seeding an erodible firebreak). However, for other negative impacts, no feasible mitigation options are available and these impacts may have to be accepted as environmental costs. The key is to find a balance between avoiding environmental damage and achieving desired treatment goals.

Soils and Water Quality

The protection and maintenance of soils and water quality can be a major issue, especially in steep terrain or in areas with highly erodible soils. There are two main concerns when treating hazardous fuels: sediment production resulting from soil disturbance, and damage to streamside management zones (riparian zones). If soil disturbance is severe enough, it can result in significant overland flow of sediment. In contrast, damaged streamside management zones can result in increases in water nutrient and stream temperature levels, and increased sediment loading in streams.

Prescribed burning itself usually does not affect water quality unless it is so intense that it consumes the duff and litter layer and exposes soils near streams. Normally, the impact of prescribed burning on erosion can be limited if burning is conducted under moist conditions so that the forest floor is not consumed completely (Swift and others 1993). However, high intensity fires can consume the entire litter layer and expose the soil to potential erosion. In addition, poorly designed firebreaks can easily become sources of erosion if placed on a slope and can facilitate water movement to a stream. Most State-level water quality best management guides address firebreak placement and construction. Thus, potential problems can usually be avoided, especially if firebreaks are re-seeded with grasses. Alternatively, the Forest Service, U.S. Department of Agriculture does not put firebreaks in wetlands; instead, the Forest Service allows prescribed burns to venture into streamside management zones and go out naturally. While it is possible to conduct a prescribed burn within a streamside management zone, care must be taken so that the area continues to perform its intended function. This means maintaining sufficient litter to slow down overland flow and avoiding excessive overstory mortality.

Mechanical operations can increase sediment production if significant soil disturbance occurs. Simply using heavy equipment will result in some soil disturbance, and mitigation (e.g., erosion fences or hay bales) may be needed. If equipment must cross perennial streams, it may be necessary to build and use temporary bridges to avoid damage to stream banks, and this can add significantly to operational costs. If a mulching treatment incorporates fuels into the soil (fig. 11), there may be increased erosion because the soil is loosened and roots have been severed. In steep areas or areas with erodible soils, the use of tracked equipment instead of wheeled machines should be encouraged since tracked equipment generally has a lower surface pressure. If properly applied, forestry herbicides have little effect on water quality if they are not applied over or near water bodies (Michael 2004). Given the limited mobility of most herbicides once in the soil, subsurface movement to water is unlikely. Because herbicides do not expose soil, erosion is unlikely unless the ground equipment used significantly disturbs the soil.

Plant Communities

The effects of forest fuels treatments on plant communities vary by treatment type and the structure of the residual (live) vegetation.

Effects of prescribed burning—The effects of an initial high-intensity prescribed burn in a forest with a heavy accumulation of fuels will differ from the effects of subsequent less intense burns. Therefore, the effects of these kinds of burns must be considered separately. If fuels are in the form of a dense understory, and fire has been excluded for some time, the first prescribed burn will likely kill most of the small hardwood, pine, and herbaceous understory, and could thermally girdle some of the midstory loblolly pines. Young saplings will probably be killed, as they will not have sufficient root reserves either to re-sprout or be competitive with older woody species also re-sprouting. Long suppressed herbaceous species will probably respond with increased growth, although they will be able to maintain this only until other vegetation in the understory starts producing a large number of leaves.

The cumulative effect of repeated prescribed burns on plant communities will depend on the timing (season) and the frequency (return interval) of the burns. If prescribed burning is repeated every 1 to 2 years, then the herbaceous layer will start to re-establish itself. For example, a long-term Forest Service experiment at Francis Marion National Forest in South Carolina compared the effects of winter prescribed burns applied at different frequencies (every 1, 2,

3, or 4 years) and found that annual and biannual prescribed burns promoted fast-growing grasses and forbs while burns at longer intervals promoted woody plants (Glitzenstein and others 2003). A South Carolina study produced similar results (White and others 1990). In Arkansas, loblolly pine stands that were burned at 3-year intervals had less understory cover than those burned at 6- or 9-year intervals (Cain and others 1998). The relationship between fire frequency and understory woody plant persistence is best thought of as a war of attrition, where root reserve levels and topkill frequency determine how long it will take to effectively eliminate the woody plants. If a prescribed burning management plan is based on burning every 3 to 5 years, the woody species will likely not be removed. Periodic burning (at a return interval of 3+ years) in either season (winter or summer) or annual winter prescribed burns can increase the number of hardwood seedlings produced by sprouting, while also reducing the number of more established but relatively small hardwood trees (Waldrop and others 1992). These findings are mainly due to the sprouting of hardwoods, such as sweetgum, from established root systems. An annual summer burning program can significantly damage the root systems of hardwood trees and keep these trees under control (Waldrop and others 1987).

Effects of mechanical treatments—The understory and midstory plant species associated with loblolly pine forests can change with different types of mechanical treatments. Phillips and others (2004) showed that distinctive plant communities can be associated with different combinations of mechanical and prescribed burning treatments. Tanner and others (1988) described reduced saw palmetto abundance, cover, and biomass for at least 3 years after drum chopping or plowing. One pass of a drum chopper can crush a plant; a second pass can sever stems from roots and lift the roots out of the ground. Tanner and others (1988) suggested that a single pass of a drum chopper during saturated soil conditions may be sufficient. However, in areas where species such as saw palmetto readily re-sprout from severed stems, a two-pass treatment may be necessary. Although some plant species readily sprout from roots and are not effectively controlled by mechanical treatments (Tanner and others 1988), a mechanical treatment that exposes mineral soil in an open-canopied pine stand could cause a change in species abundance or diversity (i.e., an increase in pine seedlings or a change in understory plant species composition).

Effects of herbicides—Some herbicide treatments can kill a large number of plants, greatly affecting the plant composition of a forest. If stem injection or granules are used, the effects may be limited to individual trees or small areas. The majority of the forestry literature on herbicide effects on plant community dynamics is based on site preparation or early release operations. These studies have shown that a single herbicide treatment usually has little effect beyond 2 years. For example, Keyser and Ford (2006) looked at the effects of applying different ratios of imazapyr and sulfometuron methyl at different loblolly pine plantations in the Virginia Piedmont during site preparation, and found that most decreases in herbaceous cover were limited to the first year. Similarly, Wilkins and others (1993a) found that while a hexazinone site preparation treatment significantly decreased cover for most woody species for at least the first 1 to 2 years, herbaceous cover was reduced for the first year on all sites and for at least 2 years in wet areas.

Invasive plants—In loblolly pine forests, there are currently two main invasive, exotic plant species of concern, cogongrass and *Lespedeza* species, that present significant wildfire hazards.

Cogongrass—A fast-growing rhizomatous grass that can quickly take over an understory (fig. 18), cogongrass is currently found mainly in coastal areas, although it has the potential to spread into uplands. It can form dense monocultures that accumulate large amounts of dry fuels. When these areas burn, the resulting fires are intense enough to kill small trees and other competitors. Since cogongrass rapidly re-sprouts after a fire, prescribed burning actually helps the species to increase its dominance. In addition, a single application of an herbicide has a limited effect on established plants, and multiple applications are needed to kill the entire root system (Faircloth and others 2006). Since cogongrass can easily grow roots from broken rhizomes, single or periodic mechanical treatments only increase its rate of spread. It takes a long-term integrated herbicide-mechanical program that is designed to exhaust root reserves to effectively eliminate this species (Jose and others 2002). If cogongrass is present in the understory, its complete elimination should be considered a priority. As with kudzu (*Pueraria montana*), a small population of survivors can quickly re-establish pretreatment levels, so a treatment program must be complete or the effort will be wasted.

Lespedeza species—Because they have densely packed leaves that contain volatile oils and the ability to re-sprout vigorously, both exotic and native species of lespedeza can form flammable clumps that can fuel high-intensity fires. At the Bankhead National Forest in Alabama, a bicolor lespedeza (*Lespedeza bicolor* Turcz.)-dominated understory was so thick that it took a mulching operation to prepare the area for prescribed burning (fig. 19). Noxubee National

Figure 18—Cogongrass (*Imperata cylindrica*) field with characteristic seed stalks. (Photo courtesy of Charles T. Bryson/Forestry Images)

Figure 19—Mulched and unmulched areas at Bankhead National Forest in Alabama with bicolor lespedeza (*Lespedeza bicolor*). (Photo courtesy of Douglas J. Marshall)

Refuge in Mississippi also has problems with clumps of exotic lespedeza, although it is an isolated problem along roads.

Other invasive plants that may cause problems in the future—Chinese tallowtree (*Sapium sebiferum*) appears to be limited to wet areas now, but it has the potential to become a pest species in upland loblolly pine forests. Although the exotic privets (*Ligustrum* spp.) can form a thick understory layer in a forest, they are usually found in moist conditions that limit the danger of wildfire. Finally, although kudzu and Japanese honeysuckle (*Lonicera japonica*) are aggressive vines, they are either limited to forest edges (kudzu) or do not normally accumulate enough fuel in the midstory to act as a fuel ladder.

Wildlife

Because loblolly pine forests are widespread and not linked to specific habitat conditions, few endangered species are specifically associated with loblolly pine. The red-cockaded woodpecker (*Picoides borealis*), although primarily associated with longleaf pine forests, can also nest in open stands of large loblolly pine trees. There is ample information about management for this species (e.g., Conner and others 2002, Masters and others 1998). The majority of birds found in southern pine forests prefer open stands with minimal midstory vegetation. Conner and others (2002) compared bird populations in open-canopy and closed-canopy loblolly pine-shortleaf pine stands. During the breeding season, species richness, abundance, and diversity were greater in open pine stands than in closed pine stands. Bird species not found in open pine stands tended to be common generalist species that required a hardwood midstory. During the non-breeding season, richness and abundance were greater in the open stands than in the closed stands, possibly grasses and shrubs were more abundant in the former. Thus, fuel reduction treatments that reduce the midstory can create an open stand structure that may be beneficial to many bird species.

For wildlife in general, there are two main concerns when fuel reduction treatments are being considered: possible loss of large snags, and possible loss of down logs. Both are common in southern fuel reduction operations and have major long-term implications for wildlife.

Loss of snags—Large snags are ecologically important because they provide nesting, roosting, and foraging opportunities for various species of wildlife. Loblolly pine forests are sub-climax communities, and unlike older forests, they do not produce many large snags over a long period.

In uneven-aged forests, snag production is usually a matter of slow but steady attrition of overstory trees. In loblolly pine forests, however, snag production is largely a bi-modal process, with high inputs during initial crown closure and then a lower rate through pine senescence during succession to a hardwood stand (van Lear 1993). However, most of the trees that die during the early crown closure are small diameter stems that have little importance as cavity sources. While they may serve as habitat for some insects, their low volume to surface area ratio (a measure of how quickly they dry out) may limit their value as insect habitat.

As the size of bird species increases, larger snags are required, which suggests that a range of snag sizes is needed to support a diverse bird community. Several papers have attempted to estimate the number of snags needed to support average-sized populations of different cavity-nesting bird species in southern pine forests. For example, Harlow and Guynn (1983) studied the availability of snags in 1- to 100-year-old pine-dominated stands in the Coastal Plain of South Carolina. Using an estimate of average bird population and assuming that cavity nesters needed three snags per year (two for breeding and one for fledglings), they determined that only 20 percent of the estimated demand for snags with d.b.h. 5 to 9 inches and only 6 percent of the demand for snags with d.b.h. ≥10 inches was being met. Harlow and Guynn (1983) hypothesized that lightning is the principle source of large snags in mature pine forests, and could produce about 0.3 large snags per acre per year. At a Piedmont site, Moorman and others (1999) found that regardless of initial snag diameter, the majority of snags fell by age six, and longevity was independent of diameter. Since most cavities were not excavated until snags reached age 6, Moorman and others (1999) suggest that snags that can be used for cavities are ephemeral and likely only usable for 1 to 2 years.

Because the production of large snags in loblolly pine forests is slow and uneven, retention of large snags in these forests may be considered a priority for wildlife management. The Forest Service attempts to retain snags for wildlife habitat, and some of its long-term management plans provide guidelines about the minimum number of snags to be retained during harvesting operations. However, snags can also be fire and safety hazards, and snag removal is often a priority item during fuel reduction operations. For example, in a 2006 mechanical mulching operation at Conecuh National Forest in Alabama, the operator was required to remove or mulch all snags over 10 inches d.b.h., as well as any snags that could fall outside the Conecuh Forest boundary. This was intended both to reduce the risk that a prescribed burn would get into the overstory and to comply with OSHA regulations. In addition, the Conecuh Forest had a red-cockaded woodpecker population and was legally required to place the protection of living cavity trees above the needs of non-endangered snag-using species. In contrast, during a mechanical mulching operation at Jones State Forest in Texas, which also had a red-cockaded woodpecker population, the only snags removed were ones deemed to be immediately hazardous to humans, and many large snags were retained.

If snags are removed during fuel reduction operations, this is likely to affect characteristics of the bird community. When snags in a 50-year-old loblolly pine plantation were removed, some secondary cavity-users, like the tufted titmouse (*Baeolophus bicolor*), the brown-headed nuthatch (*Sitta pusilla*), and the Carolina chickadee (*Poecile carolinensis*), were able to use alternate sites (dead limbs, stumps, and crevices); but the great crested flycatcher (*Myiarchus crinitus*) was not (Lohr and others 2002). Insectivorous birds may decline also since snags also represent a feeding site, although loss of fallen logs has more impact.

Down logs—While the loss of snags mostly affects cavity-using birds, the loss of down logs impacts many vertebrate species and can cause a cascade effect of species loss. Unfortunately, down logs are often targets of mulching and prescribed burning operations that are intended to reduce fuel levels. Lohr and others (2002) found that the loss of down logs had minimal impact on most non-breeding birds, which tended to be foliage gleaners. However, abundance of breeding birds was reduced by almost 50 percent and species richness of breeding birds decreased 45 percent. These breeding birds species tended to rely on insects associated with down coarse woody debris and on the additional forest structure that the woody debris provided.

Many herpetofauna (amphibians and reptiles) are also negatively affected by a loss of down logs. Since logs are insulated, they form a gradient of temperatures from warm sunlit sides to cooler areas under the log (Whiles and Grubaugh 1993). Herpetofauna use this gradient to find the best place to lay their eggs or sun themselves and may use logs as hibernation sites. In addition, down logs contain many insects and are a valuable feeding area.

The presence of a thick litter layer can reduce the need for down logs for some species. Salamanders tend to have limited ranges and narrow microhabitat needs. Since Ambystomatid salamanders use underground burrows, they may survive without down logs if the litter layer is thick enough to keep the ground cool and moist. For example, Moseley and others (2004) found that mole salamanders

(*Ambystoma talpoideum*) were not negatively affected by the removal of most down logs and pine litter in a 50-year-old loblolly pine stand as long as enough litter remained to buffer temperatures and humidity in burrows. In contrast, they found that Plethodontid salamanders require down logs for burrows and cannot use tunnels as substitutes.

Larger mammals that utilize loblolly pine forests are mostly wide-ranging generalists, and disturbance tends to increase forage and prey production in early successional habitat. In contrast, smaller mammals such as rodents can be affected by loss of down logs, especially if they are insectivores or use down logs for some portion of their life cycle. Loeb (1999) suggested that large gap formation probably reduces small mammal populations initially, but that the presence of down logs helps populations to recover. However, looking at the six most common small mammals in young loblolly pine stands, Mengak and Guynn (2003) found no obvious habitat preferences, and suggested that small mammal habitats are complex combinations of multiple microhabitats. For example, while down logs may be an important factor for golden mice (*Ochrotomys nuttalli*) and cotton mice (*Peromyscus gossypinus*), different factors influence other species. McCay and Komoroski (2004) examined the impact on shrew populations of removing all logs ≥ 4 inches diameter in loblolly pine plantations. They found that the southern short-tailed shrew (*Blarina carolinensis*) and southeastern shrew (*Sorex longirostris*) were unaffected by the loss of down logs, but that the least shrew (*Cryptotis parva*) did decline, possibly due to low initial population levels. Mengak and Guynn (2003) predicted that activities such as thinning would mostly benefit small mammals since they encourage understory growth, whereas mid-rotation burning would negatively affect small mammals by reducing woody shrubs.

Public Relations and Treatments

When conducting fuel treatments, it is important to consider the impacts of operations on other people and their activities inside and outside the forest. Land managers have the professional obligation to ensure that their operations do not endanger the public or cause unnecessary inconvenience. In addition, maintaining good relations with neighbors is a necessary requirement of land management. In many cases, the media and public will tolerate inconvenience but will not tolerate being uninformed.

Movement of heavy equipment into and out of operational areas can disrupt road traffic, inconveniencing local residents. Steps must be taken to prevent or minimize such inconvenience. In the case of rural operations, consideration may be limited to ensuring that clay or gravel is not left on paved roads during or after treatment. In areas where roads may be narrow and turn-outs limited, traffic management is vital to ensure that residents remain supportive of the activity. Another consideration that may be less obvious is noise control and the timing of work. In order to maximize productivity, contractors tend to start operations early in the day, and the noise of mechanical operations can become an issue in the wildland-urban interface. While restrictions can be placed on operations so that they do not start until a reasonable hour, contractors may not be willing to work under such conditions since lost productivity may translate into financial losses. In contrast, ground-based herbicide operations may have little impact on traffic and produce little noise. However, good public relations is very important when herbicides are used, as many people have negative attitudes about herbicides and as misconceptions about the effects of herbicides on neighboring yards or streams can damage public support for fuel reduction work.

The offsite effects of prescribed burning are heavily regulated, and a burn manager would be expected to account for them when planning a prescribed burn. A more subtle aspect of managing offsite effects is the long-term commitment needed for a permanent burning program and whether this commitment is shared by the neighbors. Unhappy neighbors can affect a burning program through complaints, and if local residents do not support a burning program, its long-term sustainability is questionable. Thus, an aggressive public relations program is a vital part of a prescribed burning regime. For example, the Bankhead National Forest in Alabama maintains a phone list of local residents to be called before a prescribed burn, in order to minimize conflict and to determine if people with health problems need to be evacuated temporarily. Similarly, Loomis and others (2001) described how a prescribed burning educational program in Florida increased public support for the practice. Miller and Wade (2003) showed how the success of a prescribed burn increased support of the program by local residents.

Fuel Reduction Impacts on Extractable Resources

A number of common extractable resources can be found in loblolly pine forests, including commercial forestry products (pulpwood and sawtimber), pine straw, mushrooms, and game species such as quail, turkey, and deer. Other nontimber forest products include floral greens, medicinal and dietary supplements, and specialty wood products (e.g., burls, twigs, branches). Because fuel treatments tend to improve access and increase the amount of herbaceous forage available, their impacts on extractable resources will

generally be favorable, although damage to overstory trees is always a possibility.

Effects on overstory pine—The understory in a loblolly pine stand has a diminishing influence on overstory growth as the trees age and increase their dominance of the site. Thus, reducing the understory by any fuel treatment method will not release the overstory from significant competition. However, crown scorch caused by a prescribed burn can reduce the crown ratio (crown length divided by tree height), which will decrease the growth rate of a tree for several years. This decrease in productivity could be compounded by losses of surface organic matter and nutrients or decreases in soil porosity (Tiedemann and others 2000). Healthy loblolly pines can replace needles lost to scorch within one to two growing seasons, but this replacement is a drain on productivity and it may take several years for growth rates to return to pre-fire levels. In addition, crown scorch is highly visible and is perceived negatively by the general public.

McInnis and others (2004) describe an experiment in which areas in two east Texas mid-rotation loblolly stands were treated with herbicide, or prescribed burned, or both. In the case of the prescribed burning treatment, subsequent growth of the overstory trees was not affected or was negatively affected, depending on the study site. The same was true for the herbicide-prescribed burn treatment. The herbicide-alone treatment did increase the growth of the overstory trees. McInnis and others (2004) suggested that the negative effects of the crown scorch were greater than any benefits derived from the herbicide treatment. Similarly, in a prescribed burned 14-year-old Piedmont loblolly pine plantation, diameter growth decreased with increasing crown scorch (Tew and others 1988). Even trees with only 0- to 3-percent scorch grew less than the controls, and Tew and others (1988) suggested that growth reductions in these trees might have been due to secondary soil factors such as root death or soil chemistry changes. However, general tree stress or damage to cambial tissues are also possible explanations. Declines were greatest during the first year, and there were no differences in diameter growth by the fourth year. Other research suggests only minor effects of crown scorch on loblolly pine growth (Waldrop and van Lear 1984). Potential pulpwood timber value may decline from bark char if buyers perceive it will reduce pulp quality.

Mechanical fuel reduction treatments can damage the bark of residual overstory loblolly pines, allowing decay agents or pathogens to enter and perhaps partially girdle affected trees. In addition, heavy equipment can injure or kill loblolly pine root systems through soil compaction or rutting.

Careful planning can reduce some of these problems, although the understory being treated may be so dense that bark injury to residual trees is inevitable.

Nontimber products—The impact of fuel reduction treatments on nontimber resources will vary. Pilz and others (2004) described how prescribed burning in Oregon affected mushroom production and suggested that fire (or lack thereof) can be used to promote different species. Many mushrooms utilize downed woody material for food, so mulching operations may encourage some species. However, treatments that reduce down wood will discourage mushroom growth. Croan (2004) evaluated the possibility of using loblolly pine wood wastes from mechanical treatments to produce gourmet and medicinal mushrooms and found that some economic species could use the material. If logs from fuels reduction treatments remain on site and are able to produce marketable mushrooms, such as shiitake (*Lentinula edodes*) or oyster (*Pleurotus* spp.), they can maintain productivity for up to 6 years (Hill 1999).

Game species—If they are conducted during certain seasons, prescribed burning and other fuel reduction treatments can adversely affect bobwhite quail (*Colinus virginianus*) populations by destroying nests and food reserves and removing vegetation that functions as nesting, roosting, or cover habitat (Maas and others 2003). However, Wilson and others (1995) showed that bobwhite quail populations can increase with stand improvement treatments (thinnings) and prescribed burning. Fuel reduction treatments that create bare patches of soil encourage the growth of herbaceous vegetation that either acts as a food source or attracts insects (Maas and others 2003). Fall, winter, or early spring treatments are recommended to avoid affecting quail during the nesting season (Moore 1957).

Prescribed burning and other fuel reduction treatments can also adversely affect eastern wild turkey (*Meleagris gallopavo*) populations by destroying food reserves and removing vegetation that functions as nesting, roosting, or cover habitat (Maas and others 2003). Annual clearing of understory by burning or other treatments is not advised for turkey management. Rather, a patchy treatment on a 2- to 4-year return interval is advised to produce the understory vegetation that is most favorable for turkey nesting and breeding. Turkey hens nest in a wide variety of habitats and select them based on the availability of adequately dense woody vegetation (Exum and others 1987). Also, turkeys consume a wide variety of foods, including insects, the seeds of numerous grasses, shrubs, and vines, and the fruit of dogwood, black cherry, and oaks (Williams and Austin 1988), and any prescribed burning for fuels management

should be scheduled so that the availability of such foods is not compromised.

White-tailed deer (*Odocoileus virginianus*) are relatively mobile and can move away from fuel reduction treatment areas and find refuge in other habitats (Ivey and Causey 1984). Deer are attracted to recently burned pine stands due to changes in food availability (Dills 1970), although pine-hardwood stands are preferred due to the exposure of acorns as a result of the treatment (Ivey and Causey 1984). Fuel reduction treatments can increase the quantity and quality of woody and herbaceous food for deer, and thus affect deer population growth, development, reproduction, and survival. Unfortunately, fuel reduction treatments can also reduce the cover necessary for escape or hiding purposes (Maas and others 2003).

Literature Cited

Abt, K.L.; Winter, S.A.; Huggett, R.J., Jr. 2002. Chapter 10: local economic impacts of forests. In: Wear, D.M.; Greis, J., eds. Southern forest resource assessment. Gen. Tech. Rep. SRS-53. Asheville, NC: U.S. Department of Agriculture, Forest Service, Southern Research Station. 635 p.

Alabama Forestry Commission. 1999. Alabama's best management practices for forestry. 5. Reforestation/stand management. http://www.forestry.state.al.us/publication/bmp/reforestations_stand_management.pdf. [Date accessed: July 25, 2006].

Alabama Forestry Commission. 2005. 2004-2005 Alabama Forestry Commission annual report. http://www.forestry.state.al.us/publication/pdfs/04-05_AFC_Annual.pdf. [Date accessed: May 25, 2006].

Arkansas Forestry Commission. 2006. Fire statistics. http://www.forestry.state.ar.us/protect/firestats.html. [Date accessed: July 25, 2006].

Bennett, B.C.; Hicklin, J.R. 1998. Uses of saw palmetto (*Serenoa repens*, Arecaceae) in Florida. Economic Botany. 52: 381-393.

Birch, T.W. 1997. Private forestland owners of the southern United States, 1994. Resour. Bull. NE-138. Radnor, PA: U.S. Department of Agriculture, Forest Service, Northeastern Forest Experiment Station. 200 p.

Bolding, M.C.; Lanford, B.L. 2005. Wildfire fuel harvesting and resultant biomass utilization using a cut-to-length/small chipper system. Forest Products Journal. 55(12): 181-189.

Boyd, R.S.; Freeman, J.D.; Miller, J.H.; Edwards, M.B. 1995. Forest herbicide influences on floristic diversity seven years after broadcast pine release treatments in central Georgia, USA. New Forests. 10: 17-37.

Boyer, W.D. 1990. Growing-season burns for control of hardwoods in longleaf pine stands. Res. Pap. SO-256. New Orleans: U.S. Department of Agriculture, Forest Service, Southern Research Station. 9 p.

Brockway, D.G.; Lewis, C.E. 1997. Long-term effects of dormant season prescribed fire on plant community diversity, structure and productivity in a longleaf pine wiregrass ecosystem. Forest Ecology and Management. 96: 167-183.

Cain, M.D.; Wigley, T.B.; Reed, D.J. 1998. Prescribed fire effects on structure in uneven-aged stands of loblolly and shortleaf pines. Wildlife Society Bulletin. 26: 209-218.

Campbell, R.S. 1948. Forest grazing work in the Deep South. In: Proceedings of the Society of American Foresters. Bethesda, MD: Society of American Foresters: 216-222.

Conner, R.C.; Hartsell, A.J. 2002. Chapter 16: Forest area and conditions. In: Wear, D.M.; Greis, J., eds. Southern forest resource assessment. Gen. Tech. Rep. SRS-53. Asheville, NC: U.S. Department of Agriculture, Forest Service, Southern Research Station. 635 p.

Conner, R.N.; Shackelford, C.E.; Schaefer, R.R. [and others]. 2002. Avian community response to southern pine ecosystem restoration for red-cockaded woodpeckers. Wilson Bulletin. 114: 324-332.

Cordell, H.K.; Macie, E.A. 2002. Population and demographic trends. In: Macie, E.A.; Hermansen, L.A., eds. Human influences on forest ecosystems: the southern wildland-urban interface assessment. Gen. Tech. Rep. SRS-55. Asheville, NC: U.S. Department of Agriculture, Forest Service, Southern Research Station. 160 p.

Croan, S.C. 2004. Conversion of conifer wastes into edible and medicinal mushrooms. Forest Products Journal. 54(2): 68-76.

Dills, G.G. 1970. Effects of prescribed burning on deer browse. Journal of Wildlife Management. 34: 540-545.

Exum, J.H.; McGlincy, J.A.; Speake, D.W. [and others]. 1987. Ecology of the eastern wild turkey in an intensively managed pine forest in southern Alabama. Bulletin Number 23. Tallahassee, FL: Tall Timbers Research Station. 70 p.

Faircloth, W.H.; Patterson, M.G.; Miller, J.H.; Teem, D.H. 2006. Wanted. Dead not alive: cogongrass. http://www.ag.auburn.edu/agrn/cogongrass/cogongrass%20fact%20sheet.htm. [Date accessed: June 15, 2006].

Fletcher, K.; Freedman, B. 1986. Effects of the herbicides glyphosate, 2,4,5-trichlorophenoxyacetic acid, and 2,4-dichlorophenoxyacetic acid on forest litter decomposition. Canadian Journal of Forest Research. 16: 6-9.

Florida Division of Forestry. 2004. Wildfire statistics for Florida: 1981-Present. http://www.fl-dof.com/wildfire/stats_fires_since1981.html. [Date accessed: June 9, 2006].

Florida Division of Forestry. 2006. Prescribed fire. http://www.fl-dof.com/wildfire/rx_index.html [Date accessed: May 25, 2006].

Frost, C.C. 1993. Four centuries of changing landscape patterns in the longleaf pine ecosystem. In: Herman, S.M., ed. Proceedings of the Tall Timbers Fire Ecology Conference, No. 18., The longleaf pine ecosystem: ecology, restoration, and management. Tallahassee, FL: Tall Timbers Research Station: 17-43.

Gagnon, J.L.; Jack, S.B. 2004. A comparison of the ecological effects of herbicide and prescribed fire in a mature longleaf pine forest: response of juvenile and overstory pine. In: Connor, K.F., ed. Proceedings of the 12th Biennial Southern Silvicultural Research Conference. Gen. Tech. Rep. SRS-71. Asheville, NC: U.S. Department of Agriculture, Forest Service, Southern Research Station. 594 p.

Georgia Forestry Commission. 1999. Georgia's best management practices for forestry. Macon, GA: Georgia Forestry Commission. 71 p.

Georgia Forestry Commission. 2006. Forest facts. http://www.gfc.state.ga.us/Resources/documents/GeorgiaForestFacts05.pdf. [Date accessed: June 9, 2006].

Glitzenstein, J.S.; Streng, D.R.; Wade, D.D. 2003. Fire frequency effects on longleaf pine (Pinus palustris P. Miller) vegetation in South Carolina and northeast Florida, USA. Natural Areas Journal. 23: 22-37.

Greene, D.W.; Harris, T.G., Jr.; DeForest, C.E.; Wang, J. 1997. Harvesting cost implications of changes in the size of timber sales in Georgia. Southern Journal of Applied Forestry. 21: 193-198.

Haines, T.K.; Busby, R.L.; Cleaves, D.A. 2001. Prescribed burning in the South: trends, purpose, and barriers. Southern Journal of Applied Forestry. 25: 149-153.

Haines, T.K.; Cleaves, D.A. 1999. The legal environment for forestry prescribed burning in the South: regulatory programs and voluntary guidelines. Southern Journal of Applied Forestry. 23: 170-174.

Hare, R.C. 1965. Contribution of bark to fire resistance. Journal of Forestry. 63(4): 248-251.

Harlow, R.F.; Guynn, D.C., Jr. 1983. Snag densities in managed stands of the South Carolina Coastal Plain. Southern Journal of Applied Forestry. 7: 224-229.

Harmon, M.E. 1984. Survival of trees after low-intensity surface fires in Great Smoky Mountains National Park. Ecology. 65: 796-802.

Harris, T.G.; Baldwin, S.; Mendell, B.C. 2005. Pulpwood and pulp: long-term history. Forest Landowner. 30(1): 50-51.

Hill, D.B. 1999. Farming exotic mushrooms in the forest. Agroforestry Note 13. Lincoln, NE: U.S. Department of Agriculture, National Agroforestry Center. 4 p.

Hughes, E. 2000. Biomass cofiring: economics, policy, and opportunities. Biomass & Bioenergy. 19: 457-465.

Husak, A.L.; Grado, S.C. 2002. Monetary benefits in a southern silvopastoral system. Southern Journal of Applied Forestry. 26: 159-164.

Ivey, T.L.; Causey, M.K. 1984. Response of white-tailed deer to prescribed fire. Wildlife Society Bulletin. 12: 138-141.

Jones, J.; Chamberlain, M.J. 2004. Efficacy of herbicides and fire to improve vegetative conditions for northern bobwhites in mature pine forests. Wildlife Society Bulletin. 32: 1077-1084.

Jose, S.; Cox, J.; Miller, D.L. [and others]. 2002. Alien plant invasions: the story of cogongrass in southeastern forests. Journal of Forestry. 100(1): 41-44.

Keyser, P.D.; Ford, V.L. 2006. Wildlife habitat and herbicides: an evaluation of a widely applied tank mix. Southern Journal of Applied Forestry. 30: 46-51.

Liechty, H.O.; Luckow, K.R.; Daniel, J.S. [and others]. 2004. Shortleaf pine ecosystem restoration: impacts on soils and woody debris in the Ouachita Mountains of the southern United States. In: 16th International Conference of the Society for Ecological Restoration. Victoria, Canada: Society for Ecological Restoration: 1-5.

Lilieholm, R.J.; Hu, S. 1987. Effects of crown scorch on mortality and diameter growth of 19-year-old loblolly pine. Southern Journal of Applied Forestry. 11: 209-212.

Litt, A.R.; Herring, B.J.; Provencher, L. 2001. Herbicide effects on ground-layer vegetation in southern pinelands, USA: a review. Natural Areas Journal. 21: 177-187.

Loeb, S.C. 1999. Responses of small mammals to coarse woody debris in a southeastern pine forest. Journal of Mammalogy. 80: 460-471.

Lohr, S.M.; Gauthreaux, S.A.; Kilgo, J.C. 2002. Importance of coarse woody debris to avian communities in loblolly pine forests. Conservation Biology. 16: 767-777.

Loomis, J.B.; Bair, L.S.; González-Cabán, A. 2001. Prescribed fire and public support. Journal of Forestry. 99(11): 18-22.

Maas, D.S.; Musson, R.L.; Hayden, T.J. 2003. Effects of prescribed burning on game species in the Southeastern United States. Champaign, IL: U.S. Army Corps of Engineers, Engineer Research and Development Center, Construction Engineering and Research Laboratory. ERDC/CERL TR-03-13. 72 p.

Mason, C.L.; Lippke, B.R.; Zobrist, K.W. [and others]. 2006. Investments in fuel removals to avoid forest fires result in substantial benefits. Journal of Forestry. 104(1): 27-31.

Masters, R.E.; Lochmiller, R.L.; McMurry, S.T.; Bukenhofer, G.A. 1998. Small mammal response to pine-grassland restoration for red-cockaded woodpeckers. Wildlife Society Bulletin. 26: 148-158.

McCay, T.S.; Komoroski, M.J. 2004. Demographic responses of shrews to removal of coarse woody debris in a managed pine forest. Forest Ecology and Management. 189: 387-395.

McInnis, L.M.; Oswald, B.P.; Williams, H.M. [and others]. 2004. Growth response of Pinus taeda L. to herbicide, prescribed fire, and fertilizer. Forest Ecology and Management. 199: 231-242.

McKee, W.H. 1982. Changes in soil fertility following prescribed burning on Coastal Plain sites. Res. Paper SE-234. Asheville, NC: U.S. Department of Agriculture, Forest Service, Southern Research Station. 23 p.

McKevlin, M.R.; McKee, W.H. 1986. Long-term prescribed burning increases nutrient-uptake and growth of loblolly-pine seedlings. Forest Ecology and Management. 17: 245-252.

Mengak, M.T.; Guynn, D.C., Jr. 2003. Small mammal microhabitat use on young loblolly pine regeneration areas. Forest Ecology and Management. 173: 309-317.

Michael, J.L. 2004. Best management practices for silvicultural chemicals and the science behind them. Water, Air, and Soil Pollution: Focus. 4(1): 95-117.

Miller, S.R.; Wade, D. 2003. Re-introducing fire at the urban/wild-land interface: planning for success. Forestry. 76: 253-260.

Mitchell, R.; Cathey, J.C.; Dabbert, B. [and others]. 2005. Managing yaupon with fire and herbicides in the Texas post oak savannah. Rangelands. 27(5): 17-19.

Miyanishi, K.; Johnson, E.A. 2002. Process and patterns of duff consumption in the mixedwood boreal forest. Canadian Journal of Forest Research. 32: 1285–1295.

Moore, W.H. 1957. Effects of certain prescribed fire treatments on the distribution of some herbaceous quail food plants in loblolly-shortleaf pine communities of the Alabama Upper Coastal Plain. In: Webb, J.W., ed. Proceedings of the Annual Conference of the Southeastern Association of Game and Fish Commissioners. 11: 349-351.

Moorman, C.E.; Russell, K.R.; Sabin, G.R.; Guynn, D.C., Jr. 1999. Snag dynamics and cavity occurrence in the South Carolina Piedmont. Forest Ecology and Management. 118: 37-48.

Moseley, K.R.; Ford, W.M.; Castleberry, S.B. 2004. Coarse woody debris and pine litter manipulation effects on movement and microhabitat use of Ambystoma talpoideum in a Pinus taeda stand. Forest Ecology and Management. 191: 387-396.

National Interagency Fire Center. 2006a. Highlights for the 2005 wildland fire season. http://www.nifc.gov/stats/summaries/summary_2005.html. [Date accessed: December 23, 2006].

National Interagency Fire Center. 2006b. 1997-2005 large fires (100,000+ acres). http://www.nifc.gov/stats/lrg_fires.html. [Date accessed: December 23, 2006].

Nelson, L.R.; Ezell, A.W.; Yeiser, J.L. 2006. Imazapyr and triclopyr tank mixtures for basal bark control of woody brush in the Southeastern United States. New Forests. 31: 173-183.

Outcalt, K.W.; Wade, D.D. 2004. Fuels management reduces tree mortality from wildfires in Southeastern United States. Southern Journal of Applied Forestry. 28: 28-34.

Perry, M.J.; Mackun, P.J. 2001. Census 2000 brief. Population change and distribution 1990 to 2000. U.S. Census Bureau, No. C2KBR/01-2. 7 p. http://www.census.gov/prod/2001pubs/c2kbr01-2.pdf. [Date accessed: Aug. 2, 2006].

Phillips, R.J.; Waldrop, T.A.; Chapman, G.L. [and others]. 2004. Effects of fuel-reduction techniques on vegetative composition of Piedmont loblolly pine-shortleaf pine communities: preliminary results of the National Fire and Fire Surrogate Study. In: Connor, K.F., ed. Proceedings of the 12th Biennial Southern Silvicultural Research Conference. Gen. Tech. Rep. SRS-71. Asheville, NC: U.S. Department of Agriculture, Forest Service, Southern Research Station. 594 p.

Pilz, D.; Weber, N.S.; Carter, M.C. [and others]. 2004. Productivity and diversity of morel mushrooms in healthy, burned, and insect-damaged forests of northeastern Oregon. Forest Ecology and Management. 198: 367-386.

Provencher, L.; Herring, B.J.; Gordon, D.R. [and others]. 2001. Effects of hardwood reduction techniques on longleaf pine sandhill vegetation in northwest Florida. Restoration Ecology. 9: 13-27.

Radeloff, V.C.; Hammer, R.B.; Stewart, S.I. [and others]. 2005. The wildland-urban interface in the United States. Ecological Applications. 15: 799-805.

Rideout, S.; Oswald, B.P. 2002. Effects of prescribed burning on vegetation and fuel loading in three east Texas state parks. Texas Journal of Science. 54: 211-226.

Rideout, S.; Oswald, B.P.; Legg, M.H. 2003. Ecological, political and social challenges of prescribed fire restoration in east Texas pineywoods ecosystems: a case study. Forestry. 76: 261-269.

Rummer, B.; Len, D.; O'Brien, O. 2004. Forest residues bundling project. New technology for residue removal. 18 p. http://www.fs.fed. us/forestmanagement/WoodyBiomassUtilization/products/bundling/ documents/bundler_report_final.pdf. [Date accessed: June 5, 2006].

Rummer, R.; Outcalt, K.; Brockway, D.; Rudolph, D.C. 2006. Mechanical mid-story reduction treatment: an alternative to prescribed fire. 9 p. Final report. Joint Fire Science Program Project 99-1-3-06. http://jfsp.nifc.gov/projects/99-1-3-06_final_report.pdf. [Date accessed: July 25, 2006].

Shea, D.J.; Bayle, B. 2006. Chapter 7: Prescribed fire management. In: Kilgo, J.C.; Blake, J.I., eds. Ecology and management of a forested landscape. Fifty years of natural resource stewardship on the Savannah River Site. Washington, DC: Island Press: 62-69.

Shepard, J.P.; Creighton, J.; Duzan, H. 2004. Forestry herbicides in the United States: an overview. Wildlife Society Bulletin. 32: 1020-1027.

Smidt, M.; Dubois, M.R.; da Silveira Folegatti, B. 2005. Costs and cost trends for forestry practices in the South. Forest Landowner. 64(2): 25-31.

Smith, W.B.; Miles, P.D.; Vissage, J.S.; Pugh, S.A. 2004. Forest Resources of the United States, 2002. St. Paul, MN: U.S. Department of Agriculture, Forest Service, North Central Research Station. 146 p.

Sparks, J.C.; Masters, R.E.; Engle, D.M.; Bukenhofer, G.A. 2002. Season of burn influences fire behavior and fuel consumption in restored shortleaf pine-grassland communities. Restoration Ecology. 10: 714-722.

Stanturf, J.A.; Kellison, R.C.; Broerman, F.S.; Jones, S.B. 2003a. Productivity of southern pine plantations. Where are we and how did we get here? Journal of Forestry. 101(3): 26-31.

Stanturf, J.A.; Rummer, R.; Wimberly, M. [and others]. 2003b. Developing an integrated system for mechanical reduction of fuel loads at the wildland/urban interface in the Southern United States [Poster]. In: Posters: technique and methods: 2nd Forest Engineering Conference. [Växjö, Sweden]: [Volume unknown]: 135-138.

Stanturf, J.A.; Wade, D.D.; Waldrop, T.A. [and others]. 2002. Chapter 25: Background paper: Fire in southern forest landscapes. In: Wear, D.M.; Greis, J., eds. Gen. Tech. Rep. SRS-53. Southern forest resource assessment. Asheville, NC: U.S. Department of Agriculture, Forest Service, Southern Research Station. 635 p.

Sun, C. 2006. State statutory reforms and retention of prescribed fire liability laws on U.S. forest land. Forest Policy and Economics. 9: 392-402.

Swift, L.W.; Elliott, K.J.; Ottmar, R.D.; Vihnanek, R.E. 1993. Site preparation burning to improve Southern Appalachian pine-hardwood stands: fire characteristics and soil erosion, moisture, and temperature. Canadian Journal of Forest Research. 23: 2242-2254.

Tanner, G.W.; Wood, J.M.; Kalmbacher, R.S.; Martin, F.G. 1988. Mechanical shrub control on flatwoods range in south Florida. Journal of Range Management. 41: 245-248.

Tew, D.T.; Jervis, L.G.; Steensen, D.H.J. 1988. The effects of varying degrees of crown scorching on growth and mortality of a young Piedmont loblolly pine. In: Miller, J.H., ed. Proceedings of the 5th Biennial Southern Silvicultural Research Conference. Gen. Tech. Rep. SO-74. Memphis, TN: U.S. Department of Agriculture, Forest Service, Southern Forest Experiment Station. 630 p.

Thill, R.E.; Martin, A., Jr. 1979. Deer and cattle diet overlap in Louisiana pine-hardwood forests: preliminary findings. Proceedings of the Annual Conference of the Southeastern Association of Fish and Wildlife Agencies. 33: 64-71.

Tiedemann, A.R.; Klemmedson, J.O.; Bull, E.L. 2000. Solution of forest health problems with prescribed fire: are forest productivity and wildlife at risk? Forest Ecology and Management. 127: 1-18.

Tsiouvaras, C.N.; Harlik, N.A.; Bartolome, J.M. 1989. Effects of goats on understory vegetation and fire hazard reduction in a Coastal forest in California. Forest Science. 35: 1125-1131.

Tyler, R.; Pongetti, J. 2006. Herbicides clear the competition. Tree Farmer. May/June 2006: 10-12.

U.S. Department of the Interior. 2006a. Healthy forests report. Washington, DC: U.S. Department of the Interior. http://www. healthyforests.gov/index.html [Date accessed: November 30, 2006].

U.S. Department of the Interior. 2006b. Healthy forests report. Washington, DC: U.S. Department of the Interior. http://www. healthyforests.gov/projects/healthy_forests_report_10_4_06.pdf [Date accessed: November 30, 2006].

U.S. Department of the Interior and U.S. Forest Service. 2006. Protecting people and natural resources: A cohesive fuels treatment strategy. Washington, DC: U.S. Department of the Interior and U.S. Forest Service. http://www.fireplan.gov/documents/cohesive_fuels_ strategy03-03-06.pdf [Date accessed: November 30, 2006].

van Lear, D.H. 1993. Dynamics of coarse woody debris in southern forest ecosystems. In: Biodiversity and coarse woody debris in southern forests. Gen. Tech. Rep. SE-194. Asheville, NC: U.S. Department of Agriculture, Forest Service, Southern Research Station. 156 p.

Varner, J.M.; Gordon, D.R.; Putz, F.E.; Hiers, J.K. 2005. Restoring fire to long-unburned *Pinus palustris* ecosystems: novel fire effects and consequences for long-unburned ecosystems. Restoration Ecology. 13: 536-544.

Wade, D.D.; Lunsford, J.D. 1989. A guide for prescribed fire in southern forests. Revised. Tech. Pub. R8-TP. Atlanta, GA: U.S. Department of Agriculture, Forest Service, Southern Research Station. 56 p.

Waldrop, T.A.; van Lear, D.H. 1984. Effect of crown scorch on survival and growth of young loblolly pine. Southern Journal of Applied Forestry. 8: 35-40.

Waldrop, T.A.; van Lear, D.H.; Lloyd, F.T.; Harms, W.R. 1987. Long-term studies of prescribed burning in loblolly pine forests of the Southeastern Coastal Plain. Gen. Tech. Rep. SE-45. Asheville, NC: U.S. Department of Agriculture, Forest Service, Southeastern Forest Experiment Station. 23 p.

Waldrop, T.A.; White, D.L.; Jones, S.M. 1992. Fire regimes for pine-grassland communities in the Southeastern United States. Forest Ecology and Management. 47: 195-210.

Wear, D.N.; Greis, J.G. 2002. The Southern forest resource assessment summary report. In: Wear, D.M.; Greis, J., eds. Gen. Tech. Rep. SRS-53. Southern forest resource assessment. Asheville, NC: U.S. Department of Agriculture, Forest Service, Southern Research Station. 635 p.

Whiles, M.R.; Grubaugh, J.W. 1993. Importance of coarse woody debris to southern forest herpetofauna. In: McMinn, J.W.; Crossley, D.A., Jr., eds. Gen. Tech. Rep. SE-94. Biodiversity and coarse woody debris in southern forests. Proceedings of the workshop on coarse woody debris in southern Forests: effects on biodiversity. Asheville, NC: U.S. Department of Agriculture, Forest Service, Southern Research Station. 147 p.

White, D.L.; Waldrop, T.A.; Jones, S.M. 1990. Forty years of prescribed burning on the Santee fire plots: Effects on understory vegetation. In: Nodvin, S.C.; Waldrop, T.A., eds. Gen. Tech. Rep. SE-69. Fire and the environment: Ecological and cultural perspectives. Asheville, NC: U.S. Department of Agriculture, Forest Service, Southeastern Forest Experiment Station. 429 p.

Wilkins, R.N.; Marion, W.R.; Neary, D.G.; Tanner, G.W. 1993a. Vascular plant community dynamics following hexazinone site preparation in the lower Coastal Plain. Canadian Journal of Forest Research. 23: 2216-2229.

Wilkins, R.N.; Tanner, G.T.; Mulholland, R.; Neary, D.G. 1993b. Use of hexazinone for understory restoration of a successionally-advanced xeric sandhill in Florida. Ecological Engineering. 2: 31-48.

Williams, L.E., Jr.; Austin, D.H. 1988. Studies of the wild turkey in Florida. Technical Bulletin No. 10. Gainesville, FL: University of Florida Press. 232 p.

Wilson, C.W.; Masters, R.E.; Bukenhofer, G.A. 1995. Breeding bird response to pine-grassland community restoration for red-cockaded woodpeckers. Journal of Wildlife Management. 59: 56-67.

Windell, K.; Bradshaw, S. 2000. Understory biomass reduction methods and equipment catalog. Tech. Rep. 0051-2826-MTDC. Missoula, MT: U.S. Department of Agriculture, Forest Service, Missoula Technology and Development Center. 156 p.

Zhai, Y.S.; Munn, I.A.; Evans, D.L. 2003. Modeling forest fire probabilities in the South Central United States using FIA data. Southern Journal of Applied Forestry. 27: 11-17.

Zimmerman, G.T.; Neuenschwander, L.F. 1983. Fuel-load reductions resulting from prescribed burning in grazed and ungrazed Douglas-fir stands. Journal of Range Management. 36: 346-350.

Appendix

Important Concepts for Understanding Fuel Treatments

In this section we discuss the general physical, biological, and ecological principles that are critical to understanding both the effects of management practices on forest fuels and the influences that these modifications will have on fire behavior and fire effects. The aim is not to provide a comprehensive treatment of these subjects, but instead to introduce a set of general concepts and definitions that are useful for understanding how fuel treatments affect fire behavior and fire severity. This information will draw on standard fire science references (Burgan and Rothermel 1984, Pyne and others 1996) as well as examples from a variety of different ecosystems to provide an introduction to fuels, fire behavior, and treatment effects.

Key Fuel Characteristics

Although fuels vary widely in their physical, biological, and chemical properties, the major influences of fuels on fire behavior can be characterized using a relatively small number of variables. The three most important of these variables are fuel load, the surface area to volume ratio of the fuel, and fuelbed depth (Burgan 1987). The fuel load represents the dry weight of live and dead fuels in an area and is normally expressed as tons per acre. Although fuel load is commonly used as an indicator of potential wildfire hazard, there is no simple correlation between fire intensity and total fuel mass. Only a portion of the total fuel load, the available fuel, will support combustion. Additionally, the size distribution and spatial arrangement of fuels strongly influence the process of combustion.

The surface area to volume ratio is a measure of how much space is enclosed by a surface. This concept is important for forest fuels since it influences how quickly moisture is gained and lost and how much energy is needed to ignite the fuel, with high surface to volume ratio fuels requiring less energy. The ratio generally decreases with decreasing fuel particle size, and is also influenced by particle shape. Fuelbed depth and fuel load together determine the compaction of the fuelbed. Expressed as the packing ratio, it is the ratio of the oven-dry fuel bulk density (computed on the basis of the total volume of the fuelbed) to the oven-dry fuel particle density. Other fuel characteristics that can affect fire behavior include chemical properties that determine heat content and flammability, physical and biological properties that affect the dynamics of fuel moisture, and horizontal and vertical spatial arrangement.

Fire Characteristics

Fire behavior is characterized using one or more metrics of fire intensity, which are defined by the physical characteristics of the fire itself. These metrics include spread rate, flame length, fireline intensity (heat production per unit length of the flaming front per second), and heat per unit area (total heat produced during the residence time of the flaming zone). As spread rate, flame length, and fireline intensity increase, fire suppression becomes increasingly difficult, and the potential for extreme fire behavior such as spotting, fire whorls, and crown fire increases. Fire severity, defined as the effects of fire on vegetation, soils, and other ecosystem properties, is a function of both fire intensity and the physical and ecological characteristics of the site. With longer flame lengths, heat is emitted higher in the forest canopy and increases the potential for crown scorch and crown fire initiation, whereas greater heat per unit areas results in a larger heat pulse and greater impact on belowground properties. These elements of fire behavior will not always respond similarly to changes in fuels. For example, a fuelbed composed of dead grasses may have a relatively high spread rate but release only a small amount of heat per unit area. In contrast, a fire burning under similar weather conditions in fuels dominated by large dead wood will have a slower spread rate, but longer flame lengths and greater heat output per unit area (Pyne and others 1996).

Predicting the effects of fuel treatments on fire behavior is challenging partly because the influence of any single fuel variable depends on other fuelbed characteristics. For example, the effects of reducing fuel loading depend on changes in fuelbed depth. Each fuelbed has an optimum packing ratio that is a function of the fuel size distribution (Burgan and Rothermel 1984). If depth remains relatively constant and packing ratio decreases below the optimum level as a result of lower fuel loads, reductions in the rate of fuel consumption and the preheating of adjacent fuel particles will lead to lower spread rates, flame lengths, and fireline intensities (Burgan 1987). In contrast, reduced loading of live fuels and large woody fuels may eliminate a significant heat sink and lead to increased fire intensity in some situations. Decreasing fuel particle size increases the surface to volume ratio of fuels, which increases the rate of combustion, decreases the need for preheating, and generally leads to higher spread rates, flame length, and fireline intensity. However, fine particles are more easily compacted than large particles, and fire intensity may be reduced if the packing ratio increases above the optimum level for a particular fuelbed.

The behavior observed in a particular fuelbed will vary as a function of weather. At any given time, only a portion of the total fuel load will be available fuels that can influence the behavior and effects of a fire. The amount of available fuel is influenced by fuel size, spatial arrangement, and fuel moisture, which vary over time with precipitation and evaporation. Different types of fuels (large versus small, live versus dead) respond to the environment at different temporal scales. Thus, it is important to understand how fuel treatments influence fire behavior over the full range of weather conditions likely to be observed at a site, which range from moderate conditions suitable for prescribed burning to extreme conditions where the potential for large, destructive wildfires is highest. For example, when live and dead fuel moistures are relatively low, rates of fire spread will be much higher in a shrub-dominated fuelbed than in compacted hardwood litter. When fuel moisture is high, fire spreads faster in compacted hardwood litter than in a shrub dominated fuelbed, although spread rates in both fuel types are relatively low (Pyne and others 1996). It is also important to recognize that vegetation also influences microclimate within a stand. Thus, treatments that modify fuels can also affect patterns of wind and fuel moisture within the fuelbed.

Fuel Types

Fuels are often organized in terms of vertical layers, which include ground fuels, surface fuels (consisting of a live and dead component), and elevated fuels (consisting of crown fuels in the forest canopy and ladder fuels that may connect the canopy with the forest floor) (Pyne and others 1996). The criterion of 6 feet is typically used to separate surface fuels from elevated fuels. A fire may be confined to a single layer (e.g., ground fire, surface fire), or may encompass multiple layers. For example, both passive crown fires (torching) and active crown fires occur in conjunction with surface fires (Scott and Reinhardt 2001). Each of these classes of fuels exhibits distinctive relationships with moisture and fire behavior, and these classes provide a convenient framework for characterizing fuels and their responses to treatments.

Ground fuels—These are located either below the soil surface or at the mineral soil-organic layer interface and include duff, organic soils, large roots, stumps, and buried logs. This layer is characterized by its tendency to produce smoldering fires that may not be readily visible as well as an important possible source of post-fire smoke. Duff is the most important ground fuel component when

hazardous fuels are to be reduced by prescribed burning or by mechanical treatments. Duff is composed of decaying organic matter in the fermentation and humus layers of the forest floor and is very important for nutrient cycling and topsoil formation. The top of the duff layer transitions into non-decomposed litter and the bottom is located at the mineral soil horizon. In loblolly pine forests that are regularly burned, little duff is produced since there is not enough accumulated litter and soil moisture to promote the process. However, in forests where fire has been excluded for decades, a significant amount of duff can form if moisture conditions permit. Tree roots tend to concentrate within the duff layer and can be destroyed if the duff burns or is compacted by heavy equipment. In contrast, in poor quality Piedmont soils with hard clay surfaces, there may be little or no duff formation due to low litter and soil moisture, past management practices, and erosion.

The distribution of other ground fuels such as roots, stumps, and logs will be highly variable both within and between sites, reflecting the history of natural disturbances and land use. Rapid fire spread through ground fuels is not normally a hazard. Organic soils (e.g., Histosols) are found in some forested and herbaceous wetlands (Varner 2004), but they are not likely to be a major concern in loblolly pine forests except in some coastal areas where former wetlands now have a loblolly pine overstory. However, a ground fuels fire with long residence time can result in mineral soil temperatures much higher than those that result from a fast moving surface fire (Hartford and Frandsen 1992). The intense and sustained heat from ground fires can result in loss of soil organic material and damage to both roots and the cambium at the base of trees (Ryan and Frandsen 1991, Stephens and Finney 2002). Smoldering combustion in the ground fuel layer presents a problem for fire suppression and prescribed burning because pockets of residual ground fire can smolder undetected for weeks and re-ignite a fire long after the initial front has passed. In addition, the large amounts of smoke produced by smoldering combustion of ground fuels can increase offsite risks associated with either wildfire or prescribed burning.

Dead surface fuels—These include litter, branches, logs, and any other dead woody material that accumulates on the surface of the ground. In addition, live plants in the surface fuel layer such as grasses and shrubs can contain dead stems and foliage. The surface area to volume ratio of dead fuels largely determines the rate at which fuel moisture is gained or lost in response to environmental change. Because most branches and stems are cylindrical in cross section, they can be classified into one of four time lag moisture classes based on average diameter. The time lag for each class represents the time needed for a fuel particle at the midpoint of the size class to reach two-thirds of the surrounding atmospheric moisture level.

The fuels in the 1-hour time-lag dead class (< 0.25 inch diameter, characterizing vegetation with a large surface-to-mass ratio) are needle and leaf litter, grasses, and small twigs. These fine fuels have the greatest influence on fire spread and are the most sensitive to short-term weather fluctuations. Fuels in the 10-hour (0.25 to 1 inch diameter) and 100-hour (1 to 3 inches diameter) time-lag dead classes are predominantly dead branches and woody stems. These larger fuels dry out more slowly than 1-hour time-lag dead fuels. Heavy concentrations of these larger fuels can retard fire spread by serving as a heat sink when their internal moisture levels are high. However, when fuel moisture is low enough, 10- and 100-hour time-lag dead fuels can burn at high intensities and for a longer time than 1-hour time-lag dead fuels. Related to the issue of fuel moisture is the position of the fuel. Barber and van Lear (1984) found that loblolly pine dead fuels on the ground decomposed 50 percent faster than elevated slash. For a few years, small branches decompose faster than larger pieces, until hardening of the branch surface occurs. There was a general decay rate of 7.2 percent, so that 50 percent of slash is lost by year 10 and 90 percent is lost by year 32.

The 1,000-hour time-lag dead fuels (> 3 inches diameter) do not influence the spread of most surface fires but can ignite under extremely dry conditions or when pre-heated by adjacent smaller fuels (Brown and others 2003). Under these conditions, fire in 1,000-hour fuels can burn at extremely high intensities, creating problems for fire suppression. Large pieces of wood, particularly those in an advanced stage of decay, can smolder for days and create problems with smoke and re-ignition. Smoldering logs can also heat soils to temperatures at which tree roots are killed. Because dead wood typically covers only a small portion of the forest floor, these effects will be spatially heterogeneous and highly localized. After major disturbances such as insect outbreaks or hurricanes, significant amounts of fuels in these larger size classes may be created. Accumulations of larger fuels have the potential to contribute a lot of smoke in a later wildfire or prescribed burn. These fuels also make suppressing a wildfire more difficult, and they may limit access or hinder construction of fire lines, thus impeding prescribed burning. After major disturbances, a short-term pulse of fine fuels may also occur, but these fuels will decompose after a few years.

Live surface fuels—These include grasses, forbs, and trees and shrubs that are less than 6 feet in height. In loblolly pine forests, herbs and grasses are most abundant following

agricultural abandonment, timber harvest, or prescribed burns. Species common in loblolly pine forests include broomsedge (*Andropogon virginicus*), ragweed (*Ambrosia artemisiifolia*), crabgrass (*Digitaria sanguinalis*), and heath aster (*Aster ericoides*) (Schultz 1997). Understory trees and shrubs can form a dense layer, particularly in open stands that are infrequently burned. Species occurring throughout the range of loblolly pine include flowering dogwood, American holly (*Ilex opaca*), hawthorn (*Crataegus* spp.), blueberry (*Vaccinium* spp.), beautyberry (*Callicarpa americana*), and viburnum (*Viburnum* spp.). Pawpaw (*Asimina triloba*), waxmyrtle, gallberry, and yaupon are also important in the Coastal Plain. While saw palmetto is common in the flatwoods of the Coastal Plain and can be a major fire hazard, it is normally not a major component of loblolly pine forests.

An important distinction between dead and live fuels is that moisture in dead fuels is controlled entirely by external weather influences, whereas moisture in live fuels is regulated by the internal physiological mechanisms of plants. Live fuels can either contribute to or retard fire behavior depending on moisture levels and the amount and spatial arrangement of dead fuels. When fuel moisture is high, live fuels serve as a heat sink and do not contribute to fire spread. When fuel moisture is low, combustion of dead fuels can readily preheat and ignite the foliage and small branches of live plants, leading to increased fire intensity. Larger branches and stems of live plants are usually not consumed by fire.

Live fuel moisture varies spatially with site characteristics and seasonally with the phenology of various plant species. Fuel moisture in deciduous woody species typically increases with leaf development in the spring and decreases once seasonal growth has been completed. Evergreen woody species typically have lower fuel moisture than deciduous species, and fuel moisture in evergreen woody species can exhibit complex seasonal trends. Moisture is most sensitive to season or weather in grasses and herbs. As fuel moisture drops below 100 percent, an increasing portion of live grasses and herbs dry out and effectively function as dead 1-hour time-lag dead fuels (Scott and Burgan 2005). When fuel moisture reaches 30 percent, live herbaceous plants become fully cured and function as dead fuels.

Ladder and crown fuels—These fuels occur at heights > 6 feet and include shrubs and trees, vines, and suspended dead foliage and branches. The vertical distribution of these fuels is a principal factor in determining crown fire risk. When live foliage is continuously distributed from the surface up to the canopy, a surface fire may propagate into the canopy and result in torching of individual trees

(Scott and Reinhardt 2001). If fire reaches the canopy, the probability of active spread is related to the bulk density of foliage and small twigs in the forest canopy, as well as the spatial continuity of tree crowns. Standing dead trees are more likely to smolder than to support flaming combustion, and are typically not considered to be ladder fuels. However, smoldering at the base of snags can weaken them and cause them to fall, creating a potential fire spread hazard if snags are located near firebreaks.

Fuel Loading and Fuelbed Structure

Immediate reduction of fuel loads can only be achieved through combustion or physical removal of fuels from a site. In most situations, prescribed burning is effective in reducing the loading of fine dead surface fuels. However, the effects of prescribed burning on fuels can vary considerably depending on the condition of the fuelbed and weather at the time of the burn. Consumption of fuel by fire generally increases with decreasing particle size and decreasing fuel moisture (Knapp and others 2005, Perrakis and Agee 2006, Scholl and Waldrop 1999, Waldrop and others 2004). Although the majority of 1-hour time-lag dead fuel is typically consumed under a wide range of burning conditions, larger sizes will be consumed only when fuel moisture is relatively low. Consumption of duff and litter also increases with decreasing moisture at the time of the burn. Prescribed burning results in widespread mortality or topkill of understory plants, but typically only the foliage and smallest branches are actually consumed, whereas larger stems become part of the dead surface fuel load.

In contrast to burning, mechanical and herbicide treatments usually redistribute fuels rather than reduce them. These effects can vary considerably depending on the type of equipment used and the management prescription applied. Thinning of overstory trees can reduce crown fire hazard by removing ladder fuels and reducing canopy bulk density. However, if residues are left untreated, higher loadings of fine dead fuels can increase the potential for high-intensity surface fires (Agee and Skinner 2005). Thus, combined treatments in which thinning is followed by prescribed burning are generally more effective than thinning alone in moderating subsequent wildfire behavior and reducing damage to overstory trees (Cram and others 2006, Raymond and Peterson 2005, Stephens and Moghaddas 2005). Although mechanical treatments have been reported to reduce fuel loading in the litter and duff layers by disturbing the forest floor (e.g., Brose and Wade 2002, Kalabokidis and Omi 1998), these findings may reflect compression of surface and ground fuels rather than an actual decrease in fuel loads (McIver and others 2003).

Other management practices such as whole-tree harvesting, physical removal of logging slash, raking fuels away from tree boles, and compaction of the surface fuelbed can also help to mitigate the effects of surface fuel accumulation after mechanical treatment (Fulé and others 2002, Jerman and others 2004, Kalabokidis and Omi 1998). Fuel compaction above the optimum packing ratio reduces the amount of oxygen available for combustion and increases the amount of heat required to propagate fire through the fuelbed (Burgan and Rothermel 1984). In addition, tightly compacted fuelbeds retain more fuel moisture and reduce effective wind speed more than loosely compacted fuelbeds. Fuels can be compacted by bulldozers or other heavy equipment that physically compresses the surface fuelbed. In ponderosa pine forests in northwestern Arizona, compression of thinning slash with a bulldozer reduced crown scorch and tree mortality in a subsequent prescribed burn (Jerman and others 2004).

Mechanical cutting and mulching of understory vegetation reduces live fuel loads and increases fuel compaction, but also increases the total loading of dead surface fuels. Mulching increases compaction of fuels by reducing fuelbed depth and increasing the observed packing ratio, and at the same time reducing fuel particle size and decreasing the optimal packing ratio. These changes should reduce spread rates through the compacted fuels, but the slow-moving fires that result can generate an extended heat pulse into the soil that exceeds the lethal threshold for plants (Busse and others 2005). In the Northeastern United States, grinding of live fuels in dogwood and catbrier (*Smilax rotundifolia*)-dominated fuelbeds reduced fire intensity in subsequent prescribed burns (Richburg and others 2004).

Spatial Patterns of Fuels

Effects of fuel treatments vary spatially within each treatment unit. The effects of prescribed burning will vary spatially depending on the heterogeneity of fuels and environmental conditions (Waldrop and others 2004). Prescribed burning conducted when overall fuel moisture is high tends to leave more unburned patches than those conducted in drier conditions (Knapp and others 2005). Mechanical operations can also result in spatial heterogeneity due to machine movement and skid trails. In some instances, slash may be concentrated in piles during mechanical operations. Spatial heterogeneity in fuels should theoretically reduce spread rates within a treatment unit, although fire severity may be higher in areas with concentrated fuels. Large diameter fuels are more likely to be consumed when they are aggregated into piles than when they are scattered. Most research on fuel treatments and fire behavior to date has considered treated areas as homogeneous units, and there is little data to support generalizations about the effects of within-stand fuel heterogeneity on fire behavior.

The vertical distribution of ladder and canopy fuels influences crown fire risk. Thinning treatments that reduce the density of smaller trees can reduce torching of individual residual trees by raising the height to the base of the live canopy. Removal of larger trees reduces the risk of active crown spread by breaking up the continuity of the canopy and reducing canopy bulk density (Scott and Reinhardt 2001). However, these modifications to the canopy fuels may be offset by other changes caused by thinning. As discussed previously, accumulations of untreated slash from thinning operations can result in increased flame lengths and fire intensities that counteract the effects of canopy fuel modifications. Furthermore, increased mid-flame wind speed and more rapid drying of fuels in open-canopied stands can also result in fire intensities higher than those observed in closed-canopy stands with similar surface fuels.

The spatial distribution of fuel treatments at a landscape scale is also an important consideration, because it will seldom be feasible to treat all areas with high fuel accumulations. Treatment locations can be prioritized by examining the spatial pattern of fuels in relation to the pattern of human populations and critical infrastructure. In general, areas that have high fire hazard and are also close to developed areas will be assigned higher treatment priorities than more isolated wildland areas (Wimberly and others 2006, Zhang 2004). Other approaches to prioritizing treatment locations use deviation from historical reference conditions as a baseline (Hann and Strohm 2003).

Once critical areas have been identified, the spatial arrangement of fuel treatments within these areas must be considered. Fuelbreaks are linear corridors within which one or more types of fuel treatments are applied. Fuelbreaks are created to give firefighters locations where they will have a better opportunity to control a wildfire, not with the expectation that the fuelbreak itself will stop a fire (Agee and others 2000). The size and location of fuelbreaks, and the treatments applied within fuelbreaks, will depend on the characteristics of the local landscape. In the South, fuelbreak placement and design is likely to be driven mostly by the interface between wildland fuels and development. Fuelbreaks located at the boundaries of developed areas are designed to protect property from fires that spread from forested areas and also protect forest resources from fires that are ignited by humans.

A complementary strategy involves the dispersal of individual treatment units across the landscape. Simulations have demonstrated that treatment of a relatively small portion of an area can reduce the spread of large wildfires, particularly if treatments are placed in a regular, rather than a random or clustered, pattern (Finney 2001, Loehle 2004). As with fuelbreaks, the expectation is not that the treatments will actually stop wildfires, but that they will reduce fire intensity enough to facilitate fire suppression. Dispersed fuel treatments, combined with other strategies such as fire-safe landscaping, may prove to be the most effective strategy in intermix areas where large numbers of dispersed structures limit the effectiveness of linear firebreaks.

In addition to their immediate effects on fuels, modifications of stand structure can also influence succession and the associated fuel dynamics. Treatments that reduce overstory canopy density also provide more resources to the forest understory, and can result in increased rates of live fuel accumulation in the surface fuel layer. However, these same treatments can reduce the rate of litterfall and dead fuel inputs from the forest overstory by reducing overstory basal area (Brender and others 1976, Johansen and others 1976).

Appendix Literature Cited

Agee, J.K.; Bahro, B.; Finney, M.A. [and others]. 2000. The use of shaded fuelbreaks in landscape fire management. Forest Ecology and Management. 127: 55-66.

Agee, J.K.; Skinner, C.N. 2005. Basic principles of forest fuel reduction treatments. Forest Ecology and Management. 211: 83-96.

Barber, B.L.; van Lear, D.H. 1984. Weight loss and nutrient dynamics in decomposing woody loblolly pine logging slash. Soil Science Society of America Journal. 48: 906-910.

Brender, E.V.; McNab, W.H.; Williams, S. 1976. Fuel accumulations in Piedmont loblolly pine forests. Res. Note SE-233. Asheville, NC: U.S. Department of Agriculture, Forest Service, Southeastern Forest Experiment Station. 4 p.

Brose, P.H.; Wade, D.D. 2002. Potential fire behavior in pine flatwood forests following three different fuel reduction techniques. Forest Ecology and Management. 163: 71-84.

Brown, J.K.; Reinhardt, E.D.; Kramer, K.A. 2003. Coarse woody debris: managing benefits and fire hazard in the recovering forest. Gen. Tech. Rep. RMRS-105. Fort Collins, CO: U.S. Department of Agriculture, Forest Service, Rocky Mountain Research Station. 16 p. http://www.fs.fed.us/rm/pubs/rmrs_gtr105.pdf. [Date accessed: June 19, 2006].

Burgan, R.E. 1987. Concepts and interpreted examples in advanced fuel modeling. Gen. Tech. Rep. INT-238. Ogden, UT: U.S. Department of Agriculture, Forest Service, Intermountain Forest and Range Experiment Station. 40 p.

Burgan, R.E.; Rothermel, R.C. 1984. BEHAVE: Fire behavior prediction and fuel modeling system—FUEL subsystem. Gen. Tech. Rep. INT-167. Ogden, UT: U.S. Department of Agriculture, Forest Service, Intermountain Forest and Range Experiment Station. 126 p.

Busse, M.D.; Hubbert, K.R.; Fiddler, G.O. [and others]. 2005. Lethal soil temperatures during burning of masticated forest residues. International Journal of Wildland Fire. 14: 267-276.

Cram, D.; Baker, T.; Boren, J. 2006. Wildland fire effects in silviculturally treated vs. untreated stands of New Mexico and Arizona. Res. Pap. RMRS-55. Fort Collins, CO: U.S. Department of Agriculture, Forest Service, Rocky Mountain Research Station. 28 p. http://www.fs.fed.us/rm/pubs/rmrs_rp055.pdf. [Date accessed: August 3, 2006].

Finney, M.A. 2001. Design of regular landscape fuel treatment patterns for modifying fire growth and behavior. Forest Science. 47: 219-228.

Fulé, P.Z.; Covington, W.W.; Smith, H.B. [and others]. 2002. Comparing ecological restoration alternatives: Grand Canyon, AZ: Forest Ecology and Management. 170: 19-41.

Hann, W.J.; Strohm, D. 2003. Fire regime condition class and associated data for fire and fuels planning: methods and applications. In: Omi, P.N.; Joyce, L.A., eds. Fire, fuel treatments, and ecological restoration: conference proceedings. Proceedings RMRS-P-29. Fort Collins, CO: U.S. Department of Agriculture, Forest Service, Rocky Mountain Research Station. 475 p.

Hartford, R.A.; Frandsen, W.H. 1992. When it's hot, it's hot… or maybe it's not! (surface flaming may not portend extensive soil heating). International Journal of Wildland Fire. 2: 139-144.

Jerman, J.L.; Gould P.J.; Fulé, P.Z. 2004. Slash compression treatment reduced tree mortality from prescribed fire in southwestern ponderosa pine. Western Journal of Applied Forestry. 19: 149-153.

Johansen, R.W.; McNab, W.H.; Hough, W.A.; Edwards, M.B. 1976. Fuels, fire behavior, and emissions. In: Mobley, H.E., senior compiler. Southern forestry smoke management guidebook. Gen. Tech. Rep. SE-10. Asheville, NC: U.S. Department of Agriculture, Forest Service, Southern Research Station. 140 p.

Knapp, E.E.; Keeley, J.E.; Ballenger, E.A.; Brennan, T.J. 2005. Fuel reduction and coarse woody debris dynamics with early season and late season prescribed fire in a Sierra Nevada mixed conifer forest. Forest Ecology and Management. 208: 383-397.

Kalabokidis, K.D.; Omi, P.N. 1998. Reduction of fire hazard through thinning/residue disposal in the urban interface. International Journal of Wildland Fire. 8: 29-35.

Loehle, C. 2004. Applying landscape principles to fire hazard reduction. Forest Ecology and Management. 198: 261-627.

McIver, J.D.; Adams, P.A.; Doyal, J.A. [and others]. 2003. Environmental effects and economics of mechanized logging for fuel reduction in northeastern Oregon mixed-conifer stands. Western Journal of Applied Forestry. 18: 238-249.

Perrakis, D.B.; Agee, J.K. 2006. Seasonal fire effects on mixed-conifer forest structure and ponderosa pine resin properties. Canadian Journal of Forest Research. 36: 238-254.

Pyne, S.J.; Andrews, P.L.; Laven, R.D. 1996. Introduction to wildland fire. New York: John Wiley. 769 p.

Raymond, C.L.; Peterson, D.L. 2005. Fuel treatments alter the effects of wildfire in a mixed-evergreen forest, Oregon, USA. Canadian Journal of Forest Research. 35: 2981-2995.

Richburg, J.A.; Patterson, W.A.; Ohman, M. 2004. Fire management options for controlling woody invasive plants in the northeastern and mid-Atlantic U.S. Final Report Submitted to the Joint Fire Science Program. Project Number 00-1-2-06. 63 p. http://www.firescience.gov/projects/00-1-2-06/00-1-2-06_final_report.pdf. [Date accessed: Nov 8, 2007].

Ryan, K.C.; Frandsen, W.H. 1991. Basal injury from smoldering fires in mature *Pinus ponderosa* Laws. International Journal of Wildland Fire. 1: 107-118.

Scholl, E.R.; Waldrop, T.A. 1999. Photos for estimating fuel loading before and after prescribed burning in the Upper Coastal Plain of the Southeast. Gen. Tech. Rep. SRS-26. Asheville, NC: U.S. Department of Agriculture, Forest Service, Southern Research Station. 25 p.

Schultz, R.P. 1997. Loblolly pine. The ecology and culture of loblolly pine (*Pinus taeda* L.). Agric. Handb. 713. Washington, DC: U.S. Department of Agriculture. [Number of pages unknown].

Scott, J.H.; Burgan, R.E. 2005. Standard fire behavior fuel models: A comprehensive set for use with Rothermel's surface fire spread model. Gen. Tech. Rep. RMRS-153. Fort Collins, CO: U.S. Department of Agriculture, Forest Service, Rocky Mountain Research Station. 80 p. http://www.fs.fed.us/rm/pubs/rmrs_gtr153.pdf. [Date accessed: July 25, 2006].

Scott, J.H.; Reinhardt, E.D. 2001. Assessing crown fire potential by linking models of surface and crown fire behavior. Res. Pap. RMRS-29. Fort Collins, CO: U.S. Department of Agriculture, Forest Service, Rocky Mountain Research Station. 59 p. http://www.fs.fed.us/rm/pubs/rmrs_rp29.pdf. [Date accessed: July 25, 2006].

Stephens, S.L.; Finney, M.A. 2002. Prescribed fire mortality of Sierra Nevada mixed conifer tree species: effects of crown damage and forest floor combustion. Forest Ecology and Management. 162: 261-271.

Stephens, S.L.; Moghaddas, J.J. 2005. Experimental fuel treatment impacts on forest structure, potential fire behavior, and predicted tree mortality in a mixed conifer forest. Forest Ecology and Management. 215: 21-36.

Varner, M. 2004. Ladder fuels (EID: 7483). http://www.forestencyclopedia.net/. [Date accessed: July 28, 2006].

Waldrop, T.A.; Glass, D.W.; Rideout, S. [and others]. 2004. An evaluation of fuel-reduction treatments across a landscape gradient in Piedmont forests: preliminary results of the National Fire and Fire Surrogate Study. In: Connor, K.F., ed. Proceedings of the 12th Biennial Southern Silvicultural Research Conference. Gen. Tech. Rep. SRS-71. Asheville, NC: U.S. Department of Agriculture, Forest Service, Southern Research Station. 594 p.

Wimberly, M.C.; Zhang, Y.; Stanturf, J.A. 2006. Digital forestry in the wildland-urban interface. In: Shao, G.; Reynolds, K.M., eds. Computer applications in sustainable forest management: Including perspectives on collaboration and integration. New York: Springer-Verlag: 201-222.

Zhang, Y. 2004. Identification of the wildland-urban interface at regional and landscape scales. Athens, GA: University of Georgia. 116 p. Ph.D. dissertation.

Acknowledgments

The following individuals have provided guidance in the development of this synthesis:

Jennifer Adams, Merritt Island National Wildlife Refuge, Titusville, FL

Stanley Anderson, Alabama Forest Commission, Montgomery, AL

Fred J. Bein, Homochitto National Forest, Meadville, MS

Greg Born, National Forests in Alabama, Montgomery, AL

Larry Capelle, Fort A.P. Hill, Bowling Green, VA

James Cherry, Croatan National Forest, New Bern, NC

Mark Clere, Ocala National Forest, Ocala, FL

Jera A. Cochran, National Forests in Alabama, Montgomery, AL

Mike Cook, Bankhead National Forest, Double Springs, AL

Jeff DeMatteis, Mississippi Forestry Commission, Jackson, MS

Dusty Dendy, Noxubee National Wildlife Refuge, Brooksville, MS

Alan Dozier, Georgia Forestry Commission, Macon, GA

William Dienst, Croatan National Forest, New Bern, NC

Kathryn Duncan, National Forests in Texas, Lufkin, TX

Michael T. Esters, National Forests in Mississippi, Jackson, MS

James Flue, National Forests in Texas, Lufkin, TX

Chris Foster, North Louisiana Wildlife Refuge Complex, Farmerville, LA

Terry Haines, U.S. Forest Service, Southern Research Station, New Orleans, LA

Dave Haywood, U.S. Forest Service, Southern Research Station, Pineville, LA

Michael Heard, Conecuh National Forest, Andalusia, AL

Patrick Hopton, Chattahoochee-Oconee National Forest, Gainesville, GA

Terri Jenkins, Savannah Coastal National Wildlife Refuges, Savannah, GA

Justice Jones, Texas Forest Service, College Station, TX

Robert Larimore, Fort Benning, Columbus, GA

Scott Layfield, Talladega National Forest, Talladega, AL

John Maitland, Fort Jackson, Columbia, SC

Don McBride, Arkansas Forestry Commission, Little Rock, AR

Helen Mohr, U.S. Forest Service, Southern Research Station, Clemson, SC

Larry Nance, Arkansas Forestry Commission, Little Rock, AR

Bill Nightingale, U.S. Forest Service, Regional Office, Atlanta, GA

Joseph O'Brien, U.S. Forest Service, Southern Research Station, Athens, GA

Brian Oswald, Stephen F. Austin State University, Nacogdoches, TX

Ken Outcalt, U.S. Forest Service, Southern Research Station, Athens, GA

Mike C. Peterson, National Forests of Alabama, Montgomery, AL

Dave Richardson, Noxubee National Wildlife Refuge, Brooksville, MS

Stanley Rikard, Fort Jackson, Columbia, SC

David Samuel, Arkansas Forestry Commission, Little Rock, AR

Carl Schmidt, Piedmont National Wildlife Refuge, Hillsboro, GA

Mary Sword-Sayer, U.S. Forest Service, Southern Research Station, Pineville, LA

G. Randall Tate, The Nature Conservancy, Atlanta, GA

Chris Thomsen, Virginia Department of Forestry, Charlottesville, VA

Larry Threet, Felsenthal National Wildlife Refuge, Dardenelle, AR

Jon Wallace, Forestry and Fire Consultant, MS

John Warner, Texas Forest Service, College Station, TX

Fred Wetzel, Okefenokee National Wildlife Refuge, Folkston, GA

Tony Wilder, Gulf Coast National Wildlife Refuge, Gautier, MS

Frank Yerby, Kisatchie National Forest, Pineville, LA

www.ingramcontent.com/pod-product-compliance
Lightning Source LLC
Chambersburg PA
CBHW080620290526
45790CB00007B/2851